A Terrible Logic

ISBN: 1-4802-5775-3
ISBN-13: 9781480257757

A Terrible Logic

S. L. Sanger

Contents

Chapter 1
Beginnings

SMITH, WILLIAM DOUGLAS, a.k.a. Bill; DOB: 5-22-53; Place of birth: Wenatchee, Washington; Race: white; Physical characteristics: height five foot nine inches, weight 175 pounds, blond hair, blue eyes, no scars or tattoos, blood type O positive; Chelan County Courts: civil file 88-3-00128-4, criminal file 92-1-00089-1; FBI: 373168PA3; Washington State DOC: 997341.

Cashmere is located in north-central Washington, a town of 3,000 or so along U.S. 2/97 next to the Wenatchee River flowing east out of the snowy Cascade Mountains. It's an arid region of the Pacific Northwest, but is green in the summer with irrigated pear, apple and cherry trees. The little town has a certain fame as the home of a fruit and nuts candy sold around the world, called Aplets and Cotlets, with a candy factory offering free samples, a lure for tourists passing through. A pretty town, its name said to be inspired by the Vale of Kashmir, blessed with views of mountains, high foothills, the river valley and offshoot canyons and plateaus abundant with fruit trees lovely in the spring with pink and white blossoms. I lived across the road from the Cashmere cemetery on the west side of town where a young woman was buried, dead of what the county coroner described as "ex-sanguination from a severed right carotid artery and right internal jugular vein due to penetrating stab wounds to the neck."

First, a little background.

You might call this the day dreaming of a couch potato. I awoke from one of my customary afternoon naps to realize, yet again, I was 64 years old and needed a score. I was on the fading memory side of a fairly undistinguished–but not quite mediocre–career as a newspaper reporter. Not a bad reporter, probably a better writer, but with small ambition, something of a clown, cynical, easily distracted. Officially, I was retired, fairly comfortably, with a middling Social Security benefit, some investment income and a paltry Hearst pension. I was going brain dead living in Bellingham, Washington, a small city on the wet side of the Cascade Mountains not far from British Columbia. I was in the gloomy damp corner of the country only because my girlfriend Toby was teaching journalism at the local community college. I was surly from lack of action. Our romance was in shoal water. I needed a viable project to replace a bag full of quixotic ideas going nowhere. I had shot my wad with one good book in print, a labor of love, a few not bad magazine articles.

Toby, an author herself, years younger than I, brimming with ideas and trying to be helpful, suggested in May 2000: "Why don't you try to do something with Bill Smith? That's an interesting story."

Naturally, since someone else had suggested it, I resisted. Slowly, though, the possibility took hold. I moved across the mountains to Cashmere, Chelan County, Washington, the picture-perfect little town along the Wenatchee River, 12 miles upstream from Wenatchee, the county seat with a population of 28,000 in 2000. A major tree fruit packing and shipping town along the Columbia River, Wenatchee called itself "the apple capital of the world." In addition, more winter pears, mostly d'Anjou and Bosc, are grown in the Wenatchee River Valley upstream from Wenatchee than anywhere else in the United States. Pear growing came to the area in the late 1800s, and Blue Star Growers, a cooperative, one of America's largest packer and shipper of winter pears, is headquartered in Cashmere

Chelan County is large, almost 3,000 square miles, with terrain ranging from high mountains at its western end, tapering down as the Wenatchee River Valley stretches from the mountains to the Columbia River on the eastern boundary. The county, population about 73,000 with a white to Hispanic ratio of three to one, has a varied economy, mostly tree fruit production and some agricultural processing, along with significant tourism involving mountain and lake resorts, ski resorts and river rafting. Lake Chelan, a very deep glacial lake 50 miles long in a jewel-like setting of mountains and orchards, is a major attraction. The Columbia River itself is an industry with its hydroelectric dams providing cheap electricity to residents, growers and factories, such as Alcoa's large aluminum smelter downstream from Wenatchee. Farther upstream is Grand Coulee Dam, one of the wonders of the world. Across the river are vast croplands, including the wheat country of the Columbia Plateau reaching to Idaho.

In September 2000, I rented a spacious apartment on Evergreen Drive across from the city cemetery, a place I was to visit often. I had lived in Cashmere once before, writing part-time for *Good Fruit Grower* magazine about the tree fruit industry, somewhat baffling at times for me after 30 years as a newspaper reporter and Associated Press writer–mostly in Seattle, Honolulu, San Francisco and Fresno, with briefer stops in Iowa City and Springfield, Ohio. When I settled in Cashmere the first time, in the summer of 1992, I vaguely knew Bill Smith was on trial in the Chelan County Court House in Wenatchee. I had a dim notion it was an open and shut case with a couple of twists, which set it apart from most criminal trials. I didn't pay much attention. Toby, who had lived near Cashmere until 1996, had brought the Smith story up in 2000 as a possible project for me because her daughter had been in kindergarten class in Cashmere with Bill and Ann Smith's youngest daughter. Toby had been slightly acquainted with Ann Smith when both had been volunteers at the elementary school. Toby's husband at the time, Rick Steigmeyer, a newspaper reporter at *The Wenatchee World* and a friend of mine, had helped cover the Smith story.

When I came to Cashmere the second time in September 2000 to begin work on what I called "the Bill Smith Project," my life became routine, not pleasant but definitely not unpleasant. I read the case documents filed in the clerk of court's office in Wenatchee, and got acquainted with the county court clerk, a rotund, dynamic woman named Siri Wood. I did interviews when possible. Not everybody likes to talk about sad or frightening events. What I enjoyed most, though, were mid-morning breaks in the courthouse café drinking coffee and eating apple fritters, reading the *Seattle Post-Intelligencer* (where I had been a reporter for 14 years) and chatting with courthouse celebrities such as the café manager, the court clerk and the county prosecutor.

In time, I was almost drowning in documents, often confused, sometimes baffled, but slowly getting a handle on the long divorce and child custody case of Smith v. Smith, which was followed in a few years by State of Washington v. William Douglas Smith.

"Reporters love murders." Calvin Trillin said in his book *Killings.* As an old reporter, I agreed. Murders are dramatic; if the murder is good enough the stories almost write themselves. But, to digress, in most jurisdictions, "murder" or "murderer" are legal terms and shouldn't be used until someone is convicted. Properly, before a conviction or unless the crime was clearly premeditated, some variation of "homicide," or "slain" is preferred, but these niceties are seldom observed by journalists. My own fussiness comes from my days as an Associated Press writer.

Murder needs a twist to last longer than a day or two as a good story. Celebrities enhance the chances, but celebrity homicides–victim or killer–do not happen often. Motives vary as do methods. Explanations or excuses also cover a wide range. Some are more plausible than others. A murder story—if it is stand out from the crowd—needs a hook, something to snag the imagination. One explanation for the grisly murder and related crimes that occurred during the chilly darkness of March 5-6, 1992, beginning in a dreary little house near the railroad tracks in the pretty little town of Cashmere, was unusually compelling. This explanation was not a legal defense, but a sensitive and almost eloquent statement, which may give the reader a quick impression of the emotional complexity involved. It was expressed not by the killer, but by his older brother, Bob Smith, at the time a 40-year-old residential irrigation system installer. It was part of a letter Bob wrote to a state investigator.

I sincerely say to you or anyone else that I do love my brother, Bill, and always will, just as I love his daughters. I make no apology for that and am not ashamed to say it. I do, however, hate what he has done and in no way want anything in this letter to be misconstrued as support or in agreement with the crimes he has committed. If this is too difficult for you or whoever to grasp or accept, then this letter has been written in vain.

"My hopes and prayers are, if nothing else, that people can somehow realize that Bill Smith is not, as a local judge has openly speculated, 'the baddest of the bad', but a man who simply got so tired of it all, let despair replace hope and now has to pay

for it the rest of his life, and has been isolated from what he loves most in this world, his four daughters.

This choice of words, "let despair replace hope," caught my attention. Here was perhaps something unusual, a story with legs.

Another view, blunt, much less-nuanced, hateful even, came from Bill Smith's mother, the biological mother he despised (he was fond of his step-mother). This opinion was part of an affidavit filed in 1988 during divorce proceedings, the Smith v. Smith segment. His mother, by then Delores C. Welch of Beaverton, Oregon, said her son Bill was an abusive father, mostly in the vocal sense, had a violent temper, often treated his wife in a demeaning manner, was racist and, in general, ruled the household with an iron hand.

Bill Smith, 24 years old, a U.S. Air Force staff sergeant, and Ann Shaw, 22, born in Northallerton, Yorkshire, England, were married in Wenatchee, Feb. 2, 1978. They had met when Bill was stationed at Royal Air Force Lakenheath in the east of England. Ann was a kitchen helper and nanny at a roadhouse called "Bull Run" near the air base. By 1986, Bill was out of the Air Force, and he and Ann were the parents of four daughters. The girls and their ages in 1986 were Colleen, 7; Tammy, 5; Kristine, 4; and Margaret, an infant, born in February. They lived in a mobile home on a small cattle ranch owned by Bill and his family in Brisky Canyon a few miles west of Cashmere. Bill was a postal clerk in Wenatchee. Ann was a housewife. Early in the morning of March 18, 1988, Ann, who was pregnant, took the four girls and fled the mobile home, with the help of friends. She left a note saying she and the girls were headed to "a safe house." A few days later, without the knowledge of her husband, she had a legal abortion. At the time, Smith said and continued to say for years that the abortion was profoundly disturbing. He told a woman friend of Ann's that his wife went "over to the coast to murder our baby." He described the abortion as "a bucket of blood with our baby ground up in it."

The divorce process was bitter, marked by disagreements concerning a parenting plan. It was an expensive process for Bill Smith, since he was the litigant with the job and decent income.

In her original divorce petition, Ann said her husband was "controlling, manipulative and extremely jealous and possessive." She accused him of constantly belittling her "opinions, feelings and accomplishments." He kept her isolated "up the canyon with the children." She gave up much of her life to keep him happy, she alleged.

"Bill can and has been sweet, charming and loving, but constantly switches from charm to anger without warning. Through the years of my marriage, I have become very fearful and intimidated by Bill." Furthermore, she said her husband was "prejudiced," especially concerning blacks and Mexicans.

(Ann Smith's divorce petition complaints echoed warnings I read in a column printed in a free throwaway newspaper. The column, "The Advice Goddess" by Amy Alkon, quoted from research in a 1993 Statistics Canada survey that listed four predictors that a woman will experience serious violence from a male partner. The danger signs: jealousy, especially talking to other men; an effort to limit contact with family members or friends; Insistence on knowing who the woman is seeing, when and where; name calling or other ways of putting a woman down or making her feel inferior.)

Ann told a friend she was shocked when Bill said he had heard on the radio that a postal worker (as he was) had killed fellow workers during a work-related rampage. "I don't blame the guy," Ann said Bill told her.

She didn't appreciate his interest in politics and public affairs. He ran for local office, was a Democratic precinct official and worked to get measures approved on the statewide ballot, such as compulsory auto insurance. She said the thousands of dollars he spent on political projects was a serious drain on their finances. "His politics came first, then his family."

Sex, in several ways, was another problem. She accused her husband of being lax about allowing his daughters to read Playboy magazine, sometimes in the bedroom with him. Once, she said, after they had separated, as proof of her sincerity to work out their differences, he asked her to spend the night with him naked. "I refused this," she said.

A male friend said "Bill was always at her," meaning he kept her pregnant.

Bill Smith shot the family dog, Ann said, after the dog accidentally bit the youngest daughter, a year old at the time, on the cheek. Ann was at the emergency room getting the daughter's left cheek stitched, and Bill shot the dog after reading a message from Ann about the incident, which she insisted had been an accident. The children loved the dog Golden very much, she said.

One piece of divorce evidence that attracted attention was a note Bill left for his wife because she was late in arriving at a post office picnic. It read:

"You stupid slimey (sic) cunt. You've fucked me over with my family, now you are fucking me with the people I work with. You are so lucky I can't get my hands on you. I hate your guts. I can't wait til the day you are dead–Bitch."

Ann said the note was written about 10 months before she fled the trailer and filed for divorce. "I think if the court reads this letter the court should have a good idea of why I am afraid of him and how he controls me and has control over the children."

Fair enough. Here is a marriage that would seem to meet the legal standard for being "irretrievably broken." Naturally, Bill Smith disputed many of his wife's arguments and provided a few of his own. He described himself as "a law-abiding citizen who has always followed the rules of the society I live in." His family had lived in the Wenatchee Valley since the 1800s and he had no intention of living anywhere else. He had a good job and was always "a loving, caring father."

In his response to the divorce petition, Bill said during the first eight years of the 10-year marriage, Ann was "a loving wife and mother." But, during the previous two years, his wife could not handle stress. She exhibited "explosive anger and rages," struck the children and experienced mood changes. The husband-wife relationship was destroyed. No more was she "a loving mommy."

"My children's childhood will be lost in a series of unhappy events" if Ann were allowed primary custody, he said. In comparison, he had a good job, family support nearby, financial stability, and he played a major role in his children's lives. The day when he came home and found his children gone on the day his wife fled "was one of the saddest times of my life."

He blamed some of his wife's alleged stress troubles on pre-menstrual syndrome, a diagnosis she partly agreed with, but she denied it was an illness.

She said the problem was under control with vitamins and diet revisions. Ever since leaving her husband, she said symptoms of PMS had vanished. In her responses to his accusations, she denied being abusive with her children, was always available to them and any depression or erratic behavior was caused by her husband's controlling behavior. "Once he didn't speak to me for three weeks."

Bitter as the divorce proceeding was, Bill Smith told me years later, he really didn't mind being divorced. His only goal at the time was to live in peace with his girls.

Later, in a 14-page letter to me in 2011, he wrote a long paragraph that seemed to be an explanation of his life, almost a testament:

"I never had a great desire to be or do anything; It use to kind of disturb me in high school that I could see no goal to want to go into a profession or channel myself into any certain career. Then, once I was married and we began having children, I was so overjoyed being a father to young little people. I loved it and them so very much. Watching them grow, protecting them, sheltering them, getting to help their young brains mature and puzzle out life day to day, was just so very rewarding. Going fishing together, playing sports together, all those things made the work and chores so worthwhile. We called ourselves "the Smith Team," and it was all so very good."

Another time, he said, "I was dumbfounded when I discovered being a parent was so much fun."

End of testament. Back to divorce court bitterness. Smith had no faith in his ex-wife as a role model for their daughters. "She (Ann) broke her leg when she was 12, and never went back to school. She never read a book. She looked at books about sewing, but never read them. He doubted that Ann was familiar with the alphabet. Her friends later disputed these comments.

Smith seldom referred to his ex-wife by name, instead calling her "my ex-wife," "she" or "the girls' mother."

"After the divorce," he said, "I looked at women as mothers first, not as girlfriends. I had plenty of girlfriends then, but women nowadays, I don't know, maybe they learned it at college or somewhere, but so many are lousy mothers." He did travel to the Philippines in 1991, he said, and married a young woman named Erma, "the best little woman I ever met," and an ideal mother possibility. Immigration delays prevented her entry into the U.S. and she has vanished from this story.

The divorce and custody dispute went to trial for four days in January 1989 before Superior Court Judge John E. Bridges. The judge decided the marriage was "irretrievably broken." No problem there. Also, no difficulty in the property settlement, with the division in line with Washington's community property laws. The parenting plan was another matter. Ann had asked for residential custody. Under an earlier temporary parenting plan, the girls had been living primarily with their father and Bill Smith fought any effort by his soon-to-be ex-wife to change his status as the live-in parent.

A child psychiatrist, Douglas J. Shadle, M.D., told the judge the three older children were abused emotionally by both parents, and abused physically by their mother. Bill Smith, he said, was directly and effectively involved with the girls' education, and their social and spiritual lives. All four girls showed affection for their father and were enthusiastic about his behavior as a parent. Ann Smith lacked confidence in her parenting skills, which resulted in frequent disputes with her daughters. One important comment, in hindsight, was that the psychiatrist said Bill Smith considered that anyone who supported Ann was involved in "humiliating" him. Shadle did not recommend any basic change in the parenting custody arrangement.

Steven F. Richardson, the attorney for the children, told the judge an atmosphere "of pure poison" characterized the parent's relationship, and there was "no doubt that Bill Smith possesses a deep-seated, vengeful hatred toward Ann Smith." He recommended a modified parenting plan, giving Ann more influence, even though he said it was clear the children preferred to live with their father. The attorney visited the Bill Smith's residence when the children were present and said "the home was clean and comfortable and the children's needs had been met." His description of Ann's apartment was similar.

The relationship between Richardson and Bill Smith also became poisonous. Smith referred to Richardson as "a leech," a term which Smith said, "probably is too kind" in view of the attorney's alleged "artistry in padding" his bill. The attorney, in a letter, complained to Smith's attorney Kyle Flick about Smith's "vulgar" comments, adding "it is my strong belief that Mr. Smith is mentally unbalanced and his demented gift of prose merely confirms that belief." In his response by letter, Smith said what Richardson took for anger "is actually disgust in your performance."

Judge Bridges' was faced with what he termed "a deplorable situation." He decided "the least detrimental alternative" was Bill Smith, even though Smith degraded the mother, was reluctant to cooperate with the court, especially with counseling orders, physically and emotionally abused his wife and exhibited a self-centered controlling influence.

But, the judge said, the father was actively involved with his children and they "related well" with him. Their mother, although making an effort to emerge from a verbally abusive and "emotionally demeaning" relationship, was overwhelmed by her children and was angered by their behavior. In spite of her immediate problems, Judge Bridges said Ann Smith showed "the future potential" to be the better parent. The judge's decision was filed April 3, 1989, and included provisions requiring counseling for the children.

This close win for Bill Smith concluded the first round of what became an even uglier and tragic four-year divorce/custody fight, ending–some said predictably–in blood. With the decision by Judge Bridges against her, Ann's attorney almost immediately filed a motion to reconsider, a process that dragged on until a second custody trial was held during April 1991 before a different judge, Charles W. Cone.

Bill Smith had filed an affidavit of prejudice against Judge Bridges, alleging the judge was "unfairly sympathetic to women's rights issues" because of his connection with the regional Rape Crisis Center and, consequently, Smith could not receive "a fair and impartial hearing." Further, Smith said the judge was influenced by his wife, Sue Clem Bridges, a county support enforcement worker. Bridges denied the allegations of unfairness, but temporarily removed himself from the case.

Judge Cone's role in the case was paradoxical. He addressed a scathing letter to both Ann Smith's attorney Chancey C. Crowell and to Bill Smith, who was acting as his own attorney. This letter summarized the custody case up to April 1991, with the comment that the current hearing was the 35th since the dissolution and parental placement dispute began in March 1988. In the eight-page letter Judge Cone sharply criticized Bill Smith's behavior, saying he had interfered with the counseling process; continued "his barrage of unfavorable comments against Mrs. Smith;" had done all in his power to frustrate Mrs. Smith's visits with the children; and had attempted to manipulate the court.

The judge said there was little hope for a solution, and "if the past is prologue," Mr. Smith will continue to disparage their mother until the children reach adulthood. In years of court appearances Mr. Smith "has never once admitted any responsibility for the troubled marriage or for violations of both the spirit and content of court orders. The judge mentioned Bill Smith's attitude about Ann Smith's supposed premenstrual syndrome.

"He treats Mrs. Smith's affliction with this condition as her being a carrier of a loathsome disease. There's no evidence in the file that he has ever been sympathetic or of assistance to her and has never recognized that the cause of this condition might be at least partially the subject of the stressful life that he imposed on Mrs. Smith during their marriage."

The judge quoted Bill Smith as stating in a court filing that "the person that wins in court is the one person that can tell the best story, to hoodwink the court into seeing matters in that party's way." The judge added that this comment is obviously a summation of Bill Smith's beliefs.

After listing these failings, Judge Cone seemed to decapitate Bill Smith's chances of winning the custody fight with this sentence: "Mr. Smith is the most egocentric, manipulative, deceptive, mendacious, selfish, unfeeling, self-centered person that this Court has had appear before it in 23 years of hearing domestic matters."

Ann Smith, Judge Cone noted, through counseling "has re-established herself as a woman, gained some self-esteem and self-confidence, has improved her appearance, has found meaningful employment and is ready to re-establish a mother-child relationship with her daughters if permitted to do so." But, he said, with Mr. Smith's guidance, "the children are encouraged to do well in school, are entered into numerous activities, are well fed and clothed and apparently satisfied with their present lot."

In what sounds like a cry of despair, the judge said the situation is one "with no solution. The courts have failed, the parents have failed, the family has failed, counseling has failed and these children will suffer for the rest of their lives … ."

Then, in a surprise twist, the judge wrote: "the best interests of the children at this time are to remain under the present parenting plan," meaning that Bill Smith remained as the primary parent. Judge Cone admitted "it is difficult to justify in law or in fact the continued placement of these children to this father, but it appears to be least damaging to a totally destructive and destroyed family. Evil wins over good. Calumny triumphs over truth. A liar prospers. Manipulation succeeds. Common sense falters. Children suffer, children suffer, children suffer."

Ten years later, during an interview after he had retired, Judge Cone told me he had left out "real good reasons I had for not allowing the children to go with the mother. The children said they would not go. They had a home, a life, good school records, chores, work, animals to care for … . What I wanted him (Bill Smith) to know was that he had not fooled me a damn bit. Of course, it didn't make any difference what you said to him. He was so manipulative. It was so necessary for him to be in total control."

After this dramatic decision, the custody case ground on, moving inexorably to its final standing, in the words of chief court clerk Siri Woods during an interview with *The Wenatchee World*, "as probably the worst (custody) case Chelan County has ever seen." The court appearance docket for Smith v. Smith, which listed such details as affidavits, motions, hearings, contempt citations, conclusions of law, court orders and decisions, ran to 11 single-spaced pages when the docket ended in 1992. Case documents were bound in five thick files, involving two trials, five judges, eight attorneys, nine counselors, more than 40 hearings and untold thousands of dollars in legal fees and fines.

Musing on a walk back to Xanadu (my nickname for my spacious Cashmere apartment) after my customary breakfast of one hotcake and black coffee at Barney's tavern and cafe, I realized how demoralized and depressed I became after reading the Smith v. Smith file at the clerk's office. Tawdry and demeaning behavior, all described in legal niceties. One obstacle after another to overcome before any issue could be resolved. Everybody was going crazy in the process with no sign of progress in anyone's life or any sense of accomplishment or hope. Constant expense, mostly for Bill Smith. Aside from all that, I was getting lost in the tangle of hearings, motions to show cause or respond to this and that, threats and counter-threats, judicial indecision and delay, and the evasive dance to avoid contempt proceedings. I couldn't figure out how to sort it out, make it readable to myself, let alone an editor or reader. My feeling was that readers don't much care about the process and want to cut to the chase, in this case meaning the bedroom, the slashed body covered by the blood-soaked once-blue blanket.

In May 1991, Smith filed an 18-page affidavit that summarized his simmering mood and rising anger at what he viewed was a system arrayed against him. He was not against counseling, he wrote, but realized its value and wished he had had some counseling when he was being raised by a "mother repeatedly tormenting her family." A divorced father, he wrote, "has no rights in divorce court. But I want to get on with my life. I have been accused of the most disgusting sexual abuse charges and investigated. I have been constantly battered in court and forced to deal with judges and lawyers. I have had my good credit intentionally destroyed. I have been physically assaulted in my home, my children have been cussed at and physically hurt by a supposedly trusted counselor and people are still trying to bankrupt me and force us out of my children's childhood home for their own greedy purposes.

"All while I am worried about paying our bills and providing for four young children and wondering how I am going to pay for three sets of braces for three sets of crooked teeth. Now I have to borrow against next year's tax return to fight a court battle over something I tried very hard to do the right thing about … ."

Bill Smith concluded his affidavit, filed in Judge Cone's court, with an ominous warning. "My children know that I will go to extraordinary lengths to protect their future, just as I have since they were babies. Every time I am attacked by the courts or Mr. Crowell (Chancey C. Crowell, Ann's attorney at the time) or their mother, it only drives them closer to me because I am the only person standing up for them."

By the end of 1991 and into early 1992, Bill Smith was nearing a boiling point over concerns about ruinous fees, mostly counseling fees, the strong possibility of being jailed for contempt of court and overall frustration with the uncertain direction of his life as a parent.

Ann Smith was gaining strength. She had remarried, to a man named Bob Patrick. She had moved to 215 Washington St., near the Burlington

Northern tracks, a house rented from Duane and Jane LaVigne, well-to-do friends and fellow members of Cashmere's United Methodist Church. Ann had a job as an assistant at the Wenatchee Valley Clinic's pharmacy in Wenatchee, partly thanks to the support of physicians who were office and house-cleaning clients. Her new husband had two daughters, girls Bill Smith described as "aggressive." Smith worried that if he lost primary custody, Ann would take his daughters to Yakima, Washington, a town more than a hundred miles away.

Bill Smith, in an affidavit, accused the new husband of threatening the Smith girls, and shouting "Soon you kids will be forced to live in my house under my rules." In contrast, Bill Smith said the 1991 Christmas with his daughters was "one of the best. We had a tree full of presents, stockings full of goodies. We had a very good year and a great Christmas."

He was afraid, with a new husband, his ex-wife would have the financial support to "overwhelm" him with legal bills. About the only bright spot was that Bill Smith said he had married recently in the Philippines, and was waiting for his bride to clear immigration and come to Cashmere to live, and be a stepmother to his girls.

The case got a different judge. Superior Court Judge T.W. "Chip" Small took over, a jurist Smith called "Smalls," and still does many years later. ("Smalls" is British slang for women's underwear.) Judge Small cited Bill Smith for contempt in early February 1992. The list of violations resulting in contempt citations was a long one, and included interfering with allowed visits of his ex-wife with her children, a fight about which parent had the children for Halloween, disagreements about counseling appointments and a dispute about speech therapy for one of the children. They fought about orthodontia care, considered by the judge to be a "major decision" in the parenting plan. Bill was ordered to serve two days in jail, scheduled for the first weekend in March. He also was ordered to pay various counseling fees in full and several hundred dollars in fines and attorney's fees for Ann Patrick. It also looked as if Bill Smith's chances for retaining his status as primary parent were losing strength, a possibility the father could not live with.

One of the last documents in the civil case Smith v. Smith was a "no show" memo from the county jail to the prosecuting attorney's office. Bill Smith had failed to show up on March 6, 1992, at the jail to begin his two-day jail time. By then "Bill Smith" had become a household name in Chelan County.

Chapter 2
Ann & Bill

Ann Smith was a slim, petite woman, with long brown hair and blue eyes. She was soft-spoken with a trace of an English accent. "An English rose," as one close friend described her. She lived with Sgt. Smith for two years in England until Bill was reassigned to Korea. He got in touch with her from America, and they were married in Wenatchee in 1978, when Bill was 24 and Ann 22. Ann's close friend in Cashmere, Rebecca Hovda, who wrote a book, *One Shot, a Thousand Holes,* about her own role in the story, said Ann had told her before the divorce that she stayed in a very unsatisfactory marriage because she had no choice. She had no independent clout; she was helpless and living up a lonesome canyon after Bill left the Air Force.

Ann Smith—no job, no training, four daughters under the age of eight, a product of a broken home, high school dropout. Marrying S/Sgt. Bill Smith, perhaps not exactly a dashing catch, but often charming, intelligent, reasonably good looking and friendly, a well-established U.S. Air Force NCO, this package must have looked attractive compared to the life she knew. She may have guessed or hoped he would fulfill her dream of escaping England and realizing a new beginning. A new beginning maybe, but not necessarily a dream fulfilled.

Do women have any idea what they are getting into when they marry? Is there some hint of trouble ahead? Do some have superior intuition and avoid the mess that trapped Ann Smith? One Cashmere wife, operating a successful business, who wanted to remain anonymous, had a simple answer. "A woman knows when marriage is a bad idea. Some do it anyway because they are helpless, vulnerable, unskilled, brainwashed, dependent. But they absolutely know marriage is a bad decision. These stories are so frequent they are almost boring."

Rebecca Hovda said Ann told her the months before she left her husband were filled with nervous tension, especially when Bill found out she was looking for an apartment. Hovda said Ann's fear "was palpable … She lived in a continual state of panic … ." When he did learn of her plans to divorce him, Ann told Hovda that Bill cried and begged her not to take the girls away. He promised he would change. "Our family is everything to him. Things are going to be better."

Hovda said she helped Ann get money for a divorce lawyer's retainer fee and the divorce procedure began, quietly. On her own, Ann Smith rented an apartment, picked up some housecleaning jobs and made arrangements for divorce papers to be served on her husband. Hovda "was shocked. She had accomplished so much on her own."

With the help of women friends, Ann reluctantly had an abortion on March 23, 1988, a few days after she filed for divorce. "Who is this person?" Hovda wondered. "Now that the tears are gone, she is all business." Ann warned Hovda that Bill knew Hovda had helped her and "he was furious." An understatement, as it turned out.

Everybody who knew her seemed to like Ann Smith, with "nice" and "pleasant" being frequent adjectives, with a cautionary "perhaps a bit subservient" thrown in. In a 1992 story in *The Wenatchee World,* a reporter quoted friends as describing her as "loving, giving, gentle, creative, strong and determined, and devoted to her four daughters." Another compliment was expressed by her pastor, the Rev. Glenn Kennedy of Cashmere's United Methodist Church. "I remember her gentle toughness," he said. "I can't tell you how many people used those words to describe her, 'gentle toughness.' "

In her book, Hovda emphasized Ann's stubborn toughness. She quoted her friend as telling her, "I want custody (of my children) so bad, but I know he'll never give up. I know he is going to make our lives a living hell."

Another transplanted young English woman, Geraldine Warner, a magazine editor and wife of Tracy Warner, editorial page editor of *The Wenatchee World,* said Ann telephoned her, probably in the summer of 1986, and invited her to tea.

Warner said Ann told her she was getting a few ex-pats together. About half a dozen women came. Bill Smith's only role was to park cars. "Ann was plain, mousy, thin, frail-looking, a person if you saw her on the street, you would not notice.

"But she must have been strong internally or she wouldn't have managed as she did. She seemed organized and orderly."

The tea was outside in the yard next to the house trailer. Scones and cucumber sandwiches, "a nice spread with tables on the lawn. Ann was sociable. Her mother was there, a nice older English woman."

Tom Corey, known as T.C. around the Wenatchee Valley, ran a repair shop in Dryden, another small town in the valley. T.C. was known for his strong interest in the opposite sex. A friend of Bill Smith's father, T.C. met Ann at a dance long after her divorce. He danced with her, liked her and wanted to get to know her better. Years later, he recalled her as "plain, but with a pleasant quality, intelligent and sensitive."

Friends said the divorce and subsequent custody fight demoralized Ann for a time, but by 1992, four years after the ordeal began, she was coming back. Seemingly stronger and more optimistic, Ann Smith married Bob Patrick, a fellow Methodist she had met at a church camp in February 1992. She moved to the little house near the railroad tracks, rented from her friends Duane and Jane LaVigne, worked hard to make the house cheerful and livable. She had a new job at the Wenatchee Valley Clinic pharmacy.

Ann Smith's friends naturally were fond of her, but so were members of Bill Smith's family. His father, Bob, Jr., had positive things to say about her and said he usually supported Ann in disputes with Bill. Bill's mother, long divorced from Bob, Jr., took her side and apparently helped her with cash.

Janice Miller, Bill Smith's aunt (his dad's sister), a retired surgical assistant, was an outspoken and articulate woman who, with her husband Erlan, had retired to an acreage on the edge of Cashmere after being away from the Wenatchee Valley much of her life. Before expressing any opinions on her nephew or his ex-wife, in an aside during a telephone conversation, she asked me if I had noticed anything different about the people of Cashmere. I replied I thought I knew what she was driving at, but asked her to tell me anyway.

"Cashmere is a closed community. People here don't like outsiders. The town sets itself apart. It reminds me of *The Stepford Wives* (a 1975 black comedy movie based on Ira Levin's best-selling novel about oddly perfect–almost robotic—wives in a small town in Connecticut). I told Mrs. Miller a cable installer had told me, when I explained what I was doing in town, "I don't think you will get much information out of the people of this Valley. They are tight-lipped people."

Mrs. Miller's remarks about the "oddness" of Cashmere residents was not the first or last time I heard similar descriptions. A man sitting at the counter of a restaurant on U.S. 2/97 in Dryden, said Cashmere was sometimes described as "the pissing post of the Wenatchee Valley." He didn't know precisely why. Another man said when people said they lived in Cashmere, the person they were talking to often said, "I'm sorry to hear that." Bill Smith intensely disliked Cashmere, once referring to the little town as "the sorry slum of Cashmere." He associated the town with a despised ex-husband of his biological mother, with so much antipathy involved that he avoided driving through the town when possible.

Smith's Aunt Judith and her husband moved to Cashmere in 1991, after Bill and Ann were divorced and the bitter child custody dispute was on the boil. They met Ann and liked her. "Ann was very outgoing and very talented, very good with her hands at sewing. She was friendly. She was a novelty in Cashmere because she was English. People were drawn to her.

"Bill called us. Ann called us. Ann was a sweet girl, maybe not as swift as some, but she was a friend. Bill, though, was my own blood and I love him and think of him as a son. It was a role hard to play. It was a conflict. Bill would call and tell me things, and Ann would call and tell me things. I couldn't repeat what one said to the other. I tried to be a calming influence," Mrs. Miller said.

"Bill had great respect for me and my husband. To him, we were the ideal couple. A long marriage and stability, things he longed for."

Another family member in conflict was Bob Smith, Bill's older brother by two years. They were only five and seven years old when their parents divorced and they were wrenched away from a reasonably pleasant life in an orchard near Dryden, and forced into a typical back and forth routine between divorced parents. They were not fond of their mother's new husband and eventually wound up living with their dad.

There were two other children, a younger brother and sister, as well as two half-brothers from the new marriage. These people do not figure in this story.

I met Bob one night in December 2000 at Xanadu No. 9 after telephone calls and an exchange of letters. Bob was a good-looking fit man of 49, still in his work clothes after a day of installing home irrigation systems. He was well spoken and talkative and said the main reason he had come by that night was to find out what I was doing and why I was doing it. I explained, probably tediously. I was an ex-reporter who had the time to explore an event I considered more than a mundane domestic tragedy, but admitted that basically, my reason was I found the story "interesting." I also mentioned to Bob that one of the most interesting single aspects was his letter to the state investigator (quoted at the beginning of this account), when Bob wrote how he loved his brother but hated what he had done, and how his brother was "a man who simply got so tired of it all, let despair replace hope … ."

I recorded the interview, but since this is not an oral history, I'll summarize. Bob started the meaty part of his comments by saying, "I might as well come out and say it. Bill and I are the two closest people in each other's lives," and added they had been best friends since they were boys.

And, about Ann: "Regardless of what anyone else will tell you, besides Bill, I knew Ann better and fuller than any other person you will talk to. I spent a lot of time with the family, and a lot of time with Ann, with her and me talking, and she told me things and talked to me about things that I know she didn't with other people."

He didn't elaborate.

"Ann and I were like brother and sister. In fact, she was closer to me than my own sister." Bob said some people think that because he stayed close to Bill, he had something against Ann. Not so. "Neither of us was happy about the situation (divorce and court fights), but we were able to still be friends."

"One word describes her, and that's 'sweet.' She was one of the nicest people I ever met."

Everybody liked Ann, everybody but Bill Smith.

Bill Smith's fan club was smaller. Opinions of Smith, sharp-featured and sharp-tongued, with an intense personality and a military bearing, varied from "weird," "wacky," and "a few bricks short of a full load" to "hard worker" and "excellent father." Even those who were not his friends generally considered him a good dad, a man whose attention was centered on his daughters. "No dummy," was the comment from a newspaper editor who had talked to him in connection with his forays into politics. The women in the office of the clerk of court agreed he was courteous and polite during his many visits to their office when he was acting as his own attorney. They also viewed him as arrogant, focused and single-minded. Some of his traits may have been connected to his military service, particularly his politeness and usually respectful attitude.

A woman neighbor of Bill Smith and his father, Bob Smith, Jr., said the dad once told her, after a squabble over fences and property lines, "If you think I'm a son of a bitch, wait until you meet my son, Bill." Some years later on the morning after Ann Smith had fled to file for divorce, the neighbor went to the Smith residence to find out what was going on. Bill Smith met her at the door and told her Ann was not home and "with absolute conviction" said: "She will pay for this!"

"That made the hair on the back of my neck stand up," she said.

The neighbor didn't want to be identified, a fairly frequent response from people who feared possible payback from Bill. She summed up her feelings: "He's smart and mean, but his girls said he made great pizza."

Some years later, in 2011, after this Smith story had traveled through more than one fork in the road, I spent a morning with Bob Smith, Jr., Bill's dad. He was 80, widowed and living on his ex-cattle ranch south of Ephrata, in the flatlands many miles east of Cashmere in what's known as the Big Bend of the Columbia River. The Cascades were visible many miles to the west. Bob, Jr. was friendly, ruddy-faced and vigorous, although not in the best of health, and very much missing his second wife, who had died not long before of leukemia. He was willing to talk about Bill, his second son.

"Bill was always a rebellious kid. After a hard spanking for some misdeed, Bill would step back, put his hands on his hips, and say, 'Well, do you feel better now?' "

Bob, Jr., for much of his working life, sold insurance in Cashmere. People told me he was a well liked and competent insurance man, low key, congenial and helpful, important characteristics in his line of work. His father had owned an orchard near Dryden and he was connected with orchards for a while. Later, Bob, Jr. "ran cattle" on acreage up Icicle Creek near Leavenworth, Washington, and on the side was "a knocker," a man who slaughtered cattle and did custom butchering. Bill helped him in this work for a time. His older son, Bob, said his dad "was stern in his own way, but he was an easy-going guy who was willing to talk with you."

Bill Smith, during a later conversation, said his dad "may have had his faults, but he never gave up on his kids." He also admired him because he was consistently "a hard worker."

Asked about Bill's divorce and court fights, Bob, Jr. said he thought the abortion "started the whole thing, the abortion and the way women helped Ann do it. Of course, you may have noticed Bill is not a woman lover." His dad figured Bill's attitudes about women likely were caused by the behavior of his biological mother, Delores. They did not get along and she was "very critical of him during the divorce and custody fight." The former Delores Smith died a few years ago. To confuse matters, Bob's beloved second wife also was named Delores.

All in all, Bob, Jr. said he was fond of Ann and often took her part during "their fusses." The father and his wife knew Ann after a visit to Bill when he was stationed in England. When Bill was reassigned to Korea, he passed through Leavenworth on leave. Bill seemed dismissive of Ann then, telling his dad when asked if Ann were still in the picture, "No, but that's the way these things work."

His dad told him, "Bill, that is not the way we do things." Bill wound up calling Ann from Leavenworth, his dad said, and proposing marriage. She accepted.

"Did I do the right thing?" his dad asked me.

"Hard to know," I replied.

More odds and ends of my chat with the dad: "Bill told me once, 'I don't need friends." The old insurance man told his son, "You can't have too many friends."

"They just cause trouble," Bill replied.

Bob said neither he nor Bill was any good at fixing anything. "We can take things apart, but we can't put them back together."

Several people, in the course of my interviewing, had wondered about Bill Smith's upbringing. Siri Wood, the Chelan County chief court clerk, said, "If I ever read a book about Bill Smith, the main thing I will want to know and the topic that would fascinate me is how he got to be the way he was. How did he grow up? I heard his upbringing was difficult and rigorous. Hard work, fire and brimstone, rigid discipline."

Nothing anybody told me indicated Bill Smith's childhood was particularly difficult. His birth mother and a subsequent husband were not listed among his favorite people, but eventually he lived with his dad, a man he respected. Hard work and discipline were included, but no mention of anything resembling "fire and brimstone."

In March 1992 the weekly *Cashmere Valley Record* ran an article quoting people who had worked with both the Smiths before and after the divorce. Most of the comments pertained to Bill Smith.

Bob Cowan, a high school teacher and baseball coach in Leavenworth, had known and coached Bill. "Very likeable … never caused any problems, small and wiry, a happy kid with a quick smile" were some of his comments. Asked about Cowan years after high school, Smith told me "good old Bob Cowan was assistant principal at the high school and a darn good basketball coach and super-good baseball coach. He was one of the very few adults I respected growing up."

Bill worked at the Peshastin lumber mill as a "planer feeder" on the night shift after leaving the Air Force. Night shift supervisor Jerry Pulse said, "Bill was a good worker–a real good worker, in fact." He also said Smith was an aggressive union shop steward who was partly responsible for causing a mill shutdown in a dispute over overtime. "He was quite set in his ways," Pulse said.

In addition to the sawmill job, Bill was taking business management classes at Wenatchee Valley College on the GI Bill and getting above average grades (he received associate degrees in business administration and management). Long after Wenatchee Valley College, Smith said he never expected to use the courses he took. The reason he went to college was because he was eligible for benefits of the GI Bill, which paid very well, so he decided to use it. He helped his parents in a custom butchering business, and tended to the 260-acre Brisky Canyon ranch, which was mostly pasture for cattle. A co-worker at the mill, Dave Lundin, told the *Cashmere Valley Record* reporter that he was amazed Bill could handle all these responsibilities. Lundin described him "as very sharp, very intelligent," a man who stood up for what he believed in. He was known for writing letters to government officials and newspapers.

After the mill closed for good, Smith went to work at the Wenatchee Post Office on the night shift, 11:30 p.m. until 8 a.m. He was a clerk, processing mail that came into Wenatchee, "breaking down" the 988 zip code for other offices, and diverting mail to individual carriers. He didn't like the job. He was employed by the postal service from 1986 until 1992. His annual salary was about $40,000.

One close friend at the post office was Al White, who said Bill Smith was "an excellent worker" and also praised his role as an attentive father, citing numerous examples of outings at Smith's Brisky Canyon ranch.

Ann Smith, soon after she was married and newly arrived from England, worked as a waitress at the Edelweiss Restaurant in Leavenworth, a town on the edge of the Cascade Mountains, once a prosperous fruit packing and lumber mill town down on its luck following various economic slumps. It revived by reinventing itself into a mock Bavarian mountain village with an emphasis on tourist attractions such as restaurants, inns and gift shops.

(This mock Bavarian theme disgusted Bill's dad, Bob, Jr., and was the reason, he said, for his move to the Big Bend Country farther east.)

The Cashmere weekly also detailed some of Ann Smith's work history. After the Edelweiss, Ann worked at an arts shop, probably around the time of her filing for divorce, followed by the abortion. She told her boss Natalie Briody that Bill was furious with her "for killing the baby." Ann was so distraught during the post-divorce custody fights that Briody "unhappily" had to let her go.

A woman named Callie Yonaka, postmistress of the Peshastin office, which is between Leavenworth and Cashmere, said Bill Smith had a reputation for being "bullheaded and self righteous." She didn't give the source of her information. Smith told me he didn't remember her exactly and never knew her, but he had a typically unflattering recollection "of some old bag" sitting at the back of the Peshastin post office. He thought Ms. Yonaka may have had him confused with his brother Bob, who "was a Peshastin guy for years."

Bill Smith after completing high school in 1971 worked at short-term odd jobs, including service station work. In a letter Smith said his best high school summer job, he said, was working for a man named John Segal on a U.S. Forest Service fire-fighting crew out of Leavenworth. The best boss he ever had, he wrote, was Dale McClain, who ran the old Columbia Market in Leavenworth, where Smith worked "doing a little bit of everything right after high school."

"Dale was a great guy, stuck to his guns, went to federal prison for his beliefs. I loved that man. Dale was defiant to the blood-suckers of the world, took his blows and proved to be more of a real American and true Westerner." I checked around for some details on McClain and learned he had been convicted on federal counts of tax evasion and firearms violations. In 1996 he was arrested on a federal charge of running the biggest meth lab ever busted in the state of Oregon. McClain died at age 66 in Lompoc, Calif., in 2009.

Smith decided during President Nixon's 1972 Christmas bombings of Hanoi to join the Air Force. He wanted to go to Vietnam, but the war was winding down by the time he completed training. Smith said he did well in the Air Force, attaining the rank of staff sergeant in fewer than four years. He completed a number of technical schools in his field, which was "fuel specialist," won awards and was well regarded by his commanding officers.

In a 2011 letter, Smith said his basic job was aircraft refueling, including liquid oxygen, and did a lot of accounting and procurement of ground fuels at overseas bases. He was a shift leader and supervised crews, spending a lot of time on the refueling ramps at air bases. His superior officers considered him competent at doing personnel evaluations, so he did frequent airmen evaluations and proficiency ratings.

He was stationed at foreign bases in Europe and Asia, mostly in England, but decided that if he wanted to have a settled life with children, he would have to leave the Air Force. His superiors, he said, urged him not to leave. "I told them there was no need for a large standing Air Force in peacetime. The really good guys would come back in if the country ever needed them."

"They gave me so much in the Air Force. Awards, decorations, education, travel, training, sports activities, so much that I cried some tears when I actually did get out after eight years. I knew that if I was going to be married and have a family that I could not stay in the military. The lifestyle was too easy and free morally to build strong family ties," he wrote in a letter to me.

His eventual job at the post office in Wenatchee was so easy he said he could "sleepwalk" through it, but it was good steady pay with benefits. He had a few friends there, but was considered "wacky" by others because of his intense attitudes about politics and union matters.

One of my most memorable interviews during the Smith project was with the late Warren Chastain, a profane and forceful man of 82. I talked to him at his dining room table in Wenatchee in June 2001. He had rented pastureland for about 20 beef cows from Smith for a year in about 1990 and got to know him fairly well, and his daughters too. "His girls fed my cows and their dad paid them."

Chastain, a big man wearing a silver dollar string tie, said he was a Marine enlisted man veteran of World War II action in the South Pacific. A sword cut by a Japanese soldier on Okinawa left an ugly scar on his left ankle. "I shot him with my pistol." He spoke of being a gold miner in California, a member of the federal security force at the Los Alamos, N.M., nuclear laboratory after the war, a juvenile officer in the sheriff's office, Stevens County, Washington, a job with the forest service and owner of a small apricot orchard.

He liked Bill Smith, but had no direct acquaintance with Ann Smith. She was long gone from Brisky Canyon by the time he rented the pasture. "I don't know why so many people disliked him. I did like him. He was abrupt at times, but he was good, and the children loved him. He treated them nicely."

In fact, his main recollections of Bill Smith were that his girls "really liked their dad and he had them with him a good share of the time, in the pickup with him a lot. You bet they liked him." Asked about any comments Bill may have made about his ex-wife, Chastain said, "He talked about her some, not a lot. He didn't rank her down too much."

How did Bill Smith strike him in general? "Something might bother him, and he would get a little angry, but not too bad. He was very protective of his kids. I heard about his wife from him, before the cutting heads off happened," Chastain said.

Chapter 3
Trial

Jury selection began Monday, Aug. 10, 1992, in the Chelan County Courthouse, Wenatchee, before Superior Court Judge Carol Wardell. Before jury selection began, however, the judge denied a defense motion for a change of venue, a motion based on pre-trial newspaper publicity. Judge Wardell did not believe selection of an impartial jury was futile "at this point." A jury of seven women and five men was chosen by midday Tuesday.

The defendant, of course, was William Douglas Smith, 38, former resident of Brisky Canyon, former postal clerk, small-time rancher and Air Force sergeant. Once he was a married man with four daughters. His old life was gone, except for his four girls, who, from now on would exist for him mostly in memory.

As he said later, he did not give his attorney, Dan Arnold, much of a case to defend. Smith was charged with first-degree murder in the stabbing death of Ann Smith Patrick, 36. In addition, he was charged with first-degree attempted murder in the nearly-fatal shotgun shootings of Rebecca Hovda, 44, and Duane and Jane LaVigne, 65 and 62, all friends of Ann Smith Patrick. All four victims lived in Cashmere and were attacked in the early morning of March 6, 1992, after they had gone to bed.

Smith pleaded not guilty by reason of insanity to all four charges.

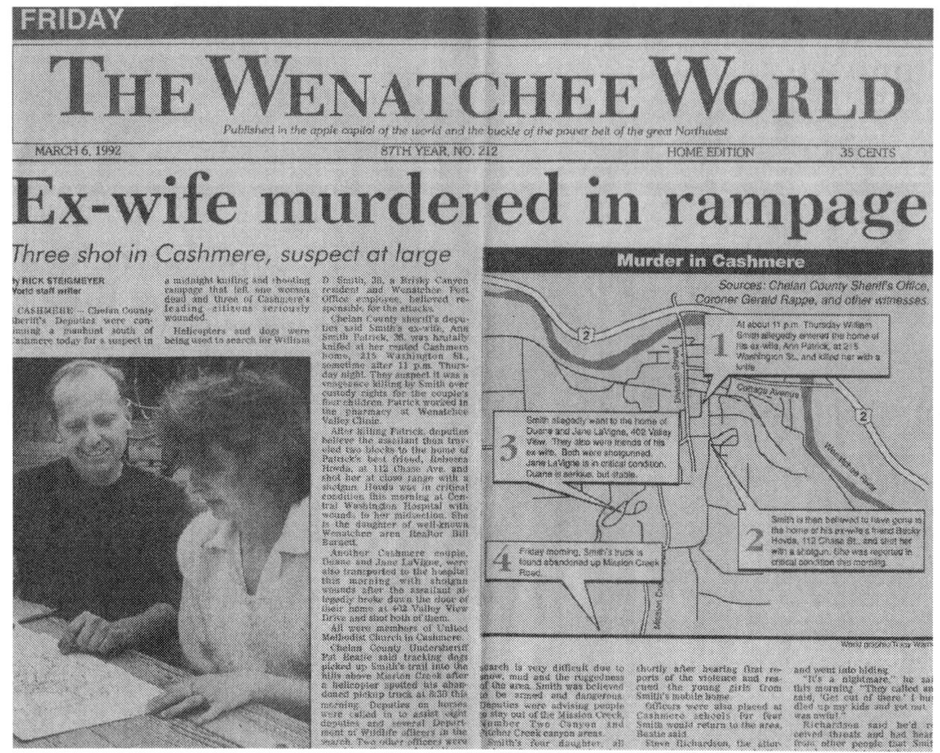

FRIDAY

THE WENATCHEE WORLD

Published in the apple capital of the world and the buckle of the power belt of the great Northwest

MARCH 6, 1992 | 87TH YEAR, NO. 212 | HOME EDITION | 35 CENTS

Ex-wife murdered in rampage

Three shot in Cashmere, suspect at large

By RICK STEIGMEYER
World staff writer

CASHMERE — Chelan County Sheriff's Deputies were conducting a manhunt south of Cashmere today for a suspect in a midnight knifing and shooting rampage that left one woman dead and three of Cashmere's leading citizens seriously wounded.

Helicopters and dogs were being used to search for William D. Smith, 38, a Brisky Canyon resident and Wenatchee Post Office employee, believed responsible for the attacks.

Chelan County sheriff's deputies said Smith's ex-wife, Ann Smith Patrick, 38, was brutally knifed at her rented Cashmere home, 215 Washington St., sometime after 11 p.m. Thursday night. They suspect it was a vengeance killing by Smith over custody rights for the couple's four children. Patrick worked in the pharmacy at Wenatchee Valley Clinic.

After killing Patrick, deputies believe the assailant then traveled two blocks to the home of Patrick's best friend, Rebecca Hovda, at 112 Chase Ave. and shot her at close range with a shotgun. Hovda was in critical condition this morning at Central Washington Hospital with wounds to her midsection. She is the daughter of well-known Wenatchee area Realtor Bill Barnett.

Another Cashmere couple, Duane and Jane LaVigne, were also transported to the hospital this morning with shotgun wounds after the assailant allegedly broke down the door of their home at 402 Valley View Drive and shot both of them.

All were members of United Methodist Church in Cashmere.

Chelan County Undersheriff Pat Beazie said tracking dogs picked up Smith's trail into the hills above Mission Creek after a helicopter spotted his abandoned pickup truck at 8:30 this morning. Deputies on horses were called in to assist eight deputies and several Department of Wildlife officers in the search. Two other officers were

search is very difficult due to snow, mud and the ruggedness of the area. Smith was believed to be armed and dangerous. Deputies were advising people to stay out of the Mission Creek, Number Two Canyon and Nahar Creek canyon areas.

Smith's four daughter, all shortly after hearing first reports of the violence and rescued the young girls from Smith's mobile home.

Officers were also placed at Cashmere schools for fear Smith would return to the area, Beazie said.

Steve Richardson, the attor- and went into hiding.

"It's a nightmare," he said this morning. "They called and said, 'Get out of there.' I bundled up my kids and got out. It was awful."

Richardson said he'd received threats and had heard from other people that Smit

Bill and Ann Smith in 1987. Photo by Tracy Warner.

Smith admitted shooting Ms. Hovda and the LaVignes at close range, but denied the attempted murder charges, saying he did not intend to kill them. He did not deny killing his ex-wife, but did not believe his act was murderous.

Gary Riesen, Chelan County's chief prosecutor since 1985, handled the state's case. A large man, friendly and congenial, Riesen, 41, was a graduate of Washington State University and Gonzaga University law school. Before becoming county prosecutor, he was in private practice in Wenatchee and had served as a Superior Court commissioner.

In his opening statement, Riesen got right to the point. "This is a case about murder. Murder–the ultimate crime. The state's evidence will show you that this is a matter fueled by vengeance and hate … This crime was planned; it was premeditated; it was intentional."

Daniel Arnold, 44, an experienced defense lawyer, hired by the county to defend Smith, disagreed totally with Riesen: "Ladies and gentlemen, these acts you have heard about in opening were done by someone who was insane at the time he committed those acts. Not psychotic or crazy or some medical term, but someone who was legally insane." He also noted that the defendant, in spite of his pleas of not guilty by reason of insanity likely would testify he is not insane, and would insist that what he did was right; it was "something he had to do."

Arnold said his client "frankly did not want to do" what he had done. "He will tell you that in order to make himself do this, he actually had to chant to himself, quietly to himself in and out, 'Save the kids." In and out, 'Save the kids.' "

These acts were not acts "of hate and vengeance," Arnold told the jury.

A little background. This 1992 case did not involve the death penalty. In Washington, the charge had to be "aggravated first-degree murder" before the death penalty was a possibility. Certain conditions had to exist before a homicide was designated "aggravated." These included, depending on the circumstances: multiple victims, or such individual victims as a law enforcement officer, prison guard, firefighter, judge, juror, attorney or news reporter. Murder for hire was another aggravation. If a first-degree murder occurred during the commission of another serious felony, it also could become a death penalty case. Riesen considered seeking death for Smith because he had broken into his ex-wife's house before he killed her, and the break-in could be considered a major felony. He decided not to, however, because he decided burglary was not Smith's main interest or motivation. If, however, one of the shotgun victims had died, the trial could have resulted in a death penalty conviction.

In her subsequent instructions to the jury regarding the insanity plea, Judge Wardell said: "Insanity existing at the time of the commission of the act charged is a defense."

For the defendant to be found not guilty by reason of insanity, she said, the jury must find that as a result of mental disease or defect his mind was affected to such an extent that he was unable to perceive the nature and quality of the crimes he is charged with committing. Or, he was unable to tell right from wrong with reference to the particular acts charged.

Another instruction informed the jurors if they found that the defendant had committed the acts charged, but was insane at the time, then they must decide if the defendant were a substantial danger to other persons unless confined or otherwise controlled.

Now, back to the trial.

Smith's testimony, which lasted two hours on Thursday, Aug. 13, came late in the trial with the case going to the jury the next day. During his testimony, the defendant forcefully and fairly skillfully presented his case for killing his ex-wife, often to the chagrin of the prosecution. His reasons for shooting her three friends were less succinct and less "logical," which is perhaps the wrong word to describe his overall motives. His day in court was his last and most public chance to publicly vent his rage at "the Chelan County system of justice" and "the slick and slide" (Smith's words) of judges and lawyers. It also was an opportunity to present the reasons for his actions, weird as these reasons may have seemed to the jury, the judge, the courtroom audience and readers of the daily *Wenatchee World,* which did a thorough job of covering the trial.

Cashmere Valley Record

Serving Cashmere, Monitor, Peshastin and Dryden

Since 1907 | Vol. 86, No. 10 | March 11, 1992 | 50 cents

Massacre harries community

Church offers solace

By Jim Davis

"We feel the depth of the tragedy to different degrees. But all of us gathered here are at least on the fringe of that pain."
-Glenn Kennedy

Glenn Kennedy

–please turn to page 6

Victims begin to recover

Smith in confinement

By Kent McCleary

Bill Smith

The legal squabbling during Smith's testimony mostly concerned a court rule, 404(b), which says, in general, that evidence is inadmissible if it pertains to alleged bad acts of the victim, in this case the late Ann Smith Patrick. It was hard to prevent Smith from alleging a litany of bad acts, in his view, committed by his ex-wife during the years of court fights over custody of the four daughters. Prosecutor Riesen thought Smith frequently stepped over the admissibility line, and Riesen's objections resulted in sessions away from the jury as the attorneys argued and Judge Wardell listened and decided how testimony was to proceed.

Bill Smith's reasons for what he did–his crimes–were rooted in his feelings for his children and his overwhelming concern that they have a happy and successful future. His testimony, however, quickly expressed his burning anger about Ann Smith's March 1988, abortion. Smith's anger continues undiminished to this day. In fact, his bitterness about the abortion was just one of several smoldering rages against the system. The newspaper reporter covering the trial wrote that Smith was usually matter-of-fact and calm, even when describing the violence. His voice became shaky, though, and he wiped his eyes when he spoke of his children.

Smith's testimony began in the usual way. He stated his name, age, education, occupation, date of marriage and divorce. These were routine. His testimony began to simmer as soon as Arnold asked how many children were included in the marriage.

"Well, there were five children. Four surviving children, and one child was killed during the marriage.

"Was that an abortion?"

"Yes, as a matter of fact. Her friends decided that."

Riesen objected, saying he did not think the answer was responsive. Judge Wardell agreed. Arnold rephrased the abortion question, but Riesen objected, saying he did not think Smith's feelings about the abortion were relevant.

"It goes to his state of mind, Your Honor … That's the primary issue here," Arnold said.

Finally, Arnold asked Smith the date of the abortion.

"My baby died on March the 23rd, 1988. My little girl would have been four years old this month."

(During the divorce proceedings, Smith had argued that since he had not been part of the abortion decision, it was illegal. It was legal in Washington. A husband's permission was not required.)

Arnold: "And your feelings about how that came about?"

"Irrelevant," objected Riesen. He was overruled this time.

Arnold: "Go ahead."

Smith: "Well, some nice ladies from Cashmere … She was taken to Seattle."

Judge Wardell: "Mr. Smith, just a minute, you need to listen to the question and only answer the questions asked … Re-ask the question, please."

Arnold: "Bill, as far as you know, how did this abortion come about?"

Smith: "Well, my ex-wife told me everything about how it came. She told me that some nice ladies in Cashmere convinced her that–because she had found out that it was going to be a baby girl rather than the possibility of a little boy–that she already had enough little girls in the house, and she didn't need to have a fifth baby girl.

"And, so they came one night, and Mrs. Hovda took her in her car to Leavenworth with my children and kept them overnight there. The next day Hovda and her children took them to the Olympic Hotel in Seattle, paid for rooms and everything, and Hovda's minister watched my kids during the daytime while Becky Hovda took Ann Smith to an abortion clinic and had my baby killed. Paid for and supported by a bunch of really nice people."

(In her book, *One Shot, a Thousand Holes,* Rebecca Hovda bitterly disputed this part of Smith's testimony. "Why can't they just shut him up? Make him stop! Why does he get to sit up there and spout lies ... Why doesn't Mr. Riesen object?")

Arnold asked for the names and ages of the daughters.

"Well, the four that are still alive: Colleen Smith, she's 13. Tammy Smith, and she's 10. Or, excuse me, she's 11 now. And Kristine is 10. And Margaret is 5–or 6, excuse me."

"And can you briefly describe your relationship with the children?"

The prosecutor objected to this question on the basis of relevancy. Arnold replied: "It goes to the heart of his case, Your Honor, his feelings about his relationship."

Judge Wardell told Arnold she did not think it went to the heart of the case, adding "I don't appreciate comments like that, but I will overrule the objection."

"Go ahead."

"How do I feel about my kids ... My children are extremely close to me. They look like me. We think a lot alike. Together, we joke; we laugh. It's very easy for me to tell my kids I love them. They're very responsive. They're very good kids. They're wonderful children. They're very, very good kids. Very smart. They do well in school. My relationship with them is very good. I can't begin to remember the last time I had to slap them or spank them or even raise my voice. Very, very good kids."

Arnold asked if there were problems with the visitation rules of the divorce agreement. Riesen objected, prompting a sarcastic, "Of course," from Smith.

Riesen's objection sparked a long argumentative session away from the jury about what was relevant and what was allowed under Rule 404(b). Riesen said the time frame was too far from the date of the crime to be relevant and the question violated the rule against introducing "bad acts" of the victim.

Arnold replied no one was trying to bring up anything "bad" about Ann Smith Patrick, but simply to show how the defendant's perceptions "of her behavior or threats from her to the children" had contributed to his alleged delusionary state of mind, i.e. insanity. Judge Wardell decided to allow the question about visitation problems if it was clear Smith's testimony was understood to be his "perception" of what happened. In addition, his testimony must be connected to subsequent testimony by psychologist Dr. R. Bruce Duthie, a witness for the defense.

Judge Wardell: "All right, are we ready to proceed?"

Arnold: "We're ready."

Riesen: "Yes, Your Honor."

Wardell: "All right. Bring the jury in."

What followed was a sparring match. Defense attorney Arnold tried to show how his client's perceptions of his ex-wife's behavior had inspired his later acts. Smith did his best to show how his ex-wife's "perceived" actions had endangered his children. Prosecutor Riesen tried hard to limit Smith's testimony to "relevance" and to Rule 404(b).

Arnold asked Smith to detail "your perceptions" of visitation problem with his ex-wife during the period 1989 to early 1992.

Smith talked about "heavy, abusive things ... choking incidents ... difficult situations." He said he had been ordered by a judge to physically force his children into his ex-wife's car and they would cry, "Daddy, daddy, don't make me go." If he let them out at his wife's address, his children would run along the side of his car, begging him to pick them up. "It was grim; it was ugly."

Hisses were heard from the audience when Smith accused his ex-wife of child abuse, which had been a main factor in the long custody fight with accusations coming from both sides.

Arnold turned to other aspects, specifically Smith's view of the litigation, the years of court fights, the back and forth, the expense, the sense of nothing getting done.

"Well, they were milking everybody for money. My ex-wife was abused more than I was ... She wasn't going to get a penny from the divorce settlement because they defrauded her. They took every dime from her. She had $32,000 coming in (from the divorce settlement). It was gone in legal fees. Everything was gone.

"We had a ranch. We had a home for the kids. Every bit of that was gone. Re-mortgaged every thing ... And then I had to represent myself, bungle through it. And her lawyers, we would go to court and the judges wouldn't even rule on nothing, but the first thing they would do is give a thousand dollars to the lawyers and say, 'Hey, we're going to pay you five thousand.' "

Smith said lawyer Steve Richardson, who was representing the children's interests, told the judge that the Smiths "don't even have money to buy toys for their kids. They don't have money to buy nothing, but Judge (John E.) Bridges gave him $5,000."

"The whole thing was to keep the parties as mad as possible and keep it in turmoil so that the money could pour in for the lawyers. And the judges were winking and making deals and slick and slide ... It was completely illegal ... there is no law." Smith said Judge (Charles W.) Cone once told him to "Shut up and sit down. I told the judges to shut up."

Smith said his ex-wife became "a vegetable" from the stress of the legal conflict. "She was exploited more than we were, and the kids lost everything. That was their childhood home and their property. It's all gone because of the court."

At this point, Riesen objected, saying he didn't think a question had been asked for quite a while. Sustained.

Arnold again brought up Smith's view that the legal system was illegal.

Smith: "Illegal? Do you think there is any law in this country? You're kidding me. I begged those guys to just let the kids have a voice. They had a right to have a say in what was happening. The psychologist said the kids should talk, and the judges denied it ... There is no law when it comes to kids. There is no law. I mean, maybe there is in some part of Afghanistan. I mean, that's bullshit."

Arnold left the Chelan County court system discussion and asked Smith to elaborate on an earlier comment that he did what he did to save his children.

"Yes, yes. It's absolutely the truth, yes."

Arnold: "And what did you mean by that?"

Smith: "I have to tell you that every time my kids left, I knew for a fact there was a good chance that I wouldn't see them again ... You're married for ten years and you tell secrets. You hear of the background of your wife's childhood and what her secret fears are ... and the threats that she makes and suicide attempts. Depression so severe ... and you worry, you know, is this the time, you know, that she's going to take care of herself? Is she going to take the kids with her?"

Smith told of walking into one of the girl's bedrooms and all four were playing with Barbie dolls. "They're combing their hair and putting their clothes on, and talking about, 'Well, yes, Mom is going to die.' "

"And, you say, 'Well, girls, you shouldn't talk about your Barbies like that.' You know, a little face will look up at me and say, 'I'm not talking about Barbie. We're talking about killing mom.' You know, how can you–you know, how can you deal with things like that?"

Smith rambles a bit, and complains about court-appointed counselors, "kooks" he called them, and said judges wouldn't allow his choices to be appointed, "professionals" who were perceptive and who would help the children. "So, nothing ever happens."

Arnold brought it back to a vital question. "What did you feel you had to do?"

"Well, it wasn't a feeling. I mean, you see that the things can't go on. Your children are zombies. They're growing into mean and angry little people. And people are exploiting the situation all the way around." The court system, he said, was encouraging the "escalating" of trouble between the parents, and trying "to manipulate" the situation so that it seemed the parents were fighting "all the time when under the surface her and I have nothing to fight about."

Any fighting, he said, was not "over the marriage. The marriage was over a long time ago. We weren't mad at each other. We couldn't figure out a way that the kids would come out of this without being totally destroyed. You can't imagine how many nights my kids would cry and cry and cry. I would hold them, and they wanted it to stop. They wanted it to stop. There was no way it could continue."

Arnold: "Bill, how did you feel about yourself, about letting this go on?"

A rambling answer followed, including the comment: "You're a divorced father; you don't have any rights. You don't have nothing to say about things. You know that you're powerless. You know that, all these things. But deep down you know you have to do something some way, some how … How I felt about things is my kids were begging me to protect them, begging me to do something. And, I was gutless because I couldn't figure out a way. I mean, strong–strong measures … to get my kids out of it, to get my kids away from the situation."

Arnold: "What did you mean by "gutless? ' "

"Well, I was condoning the position the judges were putting me in. I was the one that they told to go load the kids in the car … and they were crying and frightened … and I had to push them out of the car and I had to drive away."

Here, another recess was called for a meeting away from the jury to get some legal procedures straight, including a stern order to the defendant to cease his frequent accusations that his ex-wife had committed "bad acts."

After the conference, Arnold again tried to get a definition of "gutless" from his client.

"I just meant that I should do something for my kids. Even though for myself, you know, it was going to be something unpleasant or something that I didn't want to do, but something that had to be done," Smith said.

Arnold: "Directing your attention to March of this year, what did you do?"

"Well, I had a lot of ideas one way or another of things that had to be done, and finally I made sure that fighting between the kids and their mom and me was over with."

That part of his testimony was clear enough. He intended to deal in a final way to end the dispute with his ex-wife. Another part of this section was not so clear, but apparently an oblique and semi-incoherent reference to his actions against Mrs. Hovda and the LaVignes. The meaning seemed tangled, in an ominous way, when he testified:

"That people I had hoped or I had expected to shelter or look after my kids and who hadn't done that who had broken–I guess I would have to call it an implied trust that my kids would be looked after when they were with my ex-wife, and it didn't happen–that they were not allowed to make any more decisions or that they were identified by one means or another of leaving my kids alone." Smith usually was more articulate, more lucid in describing his motives and actions.

(Years later, he was blunt and abundantly clear when he told me his reason for shooting Mrs. Hovda and the LaVignes was "to leave a mark on them" so they would remember "somebody was mad about their treatment of my kids. I wanted them to know their behavior was bad. I shot so that every day they would see that mark I made." He still denied he intended to kill them.)

Arnold continued: "Bill, you finally took some final action in this, did you not?"

"Yes, I went through a long process of days and days where nothing–nothing was working out ... and it was a lot of hard thinking. A lot of trying to face the facts ... "

Arnold asked him if he came to a conclusion.

"Well, there really wasn't really no conclusion ... I finally was faced with the fact that I had do something, that I had to–that there was no more time. That everything was gone ... and I was out of time. There was–I was just flat–flat out of time."

Arnold asked: "What day was that?"

"That was the fifth of March, the night of the fifth of March."

"All right. And what did you do that night, the fifth of March?"

"That was one of my days off, and I had spent the day (a Thursday) taking care of my kids, and everything was so good." Smith was to begin serving the two-day jail sentence for contempt of court the next day. He took in a school basketball game and watched his oldest girl play. He fed his children and helped them with their homework.

"And Margaret (at six, the youngest) was nervous about the next night (when the girls were to stay with their mother), and it was time for her to go to bed, and she asked me to come lay down with her for a while, which I did, and she finally went to sleep. And I got the other kids to bed, and just kept thinking what good kids they were and sat down and tried to write. And I would go to the kids' bedrooms and check on them, and I just knew that it couldn't go on, you know, even one more day. And I just had to, you know, find a way somehow to help them."

(Also, years later, Smith told me each girl came to him that night, separately, and told him they would not go to their mother's the next day.)

He sat at the kitchen table for hours "crying, trying to do work, paperwork and writing. I couldn't see any way that anything was going to work out. Finally, about midnight I just decided that it was too important, that it was–it was just too good, that my kids were worth it. That it was–That it was important enough for me to do whatever it took to see that they were going to be taken care of."

Smith got up and went to a hall closet where he kept a hunting pack and several guns. He took his 20-gauge single-shot shotgun outside and sawed off the end of the barrel, which he said would make it less powerful, a notion which Smith realized later was "a huge miscalculation."

(Testimony later from Gaylan Warren, a ballistics expert formerly with the Washington State Patrol crime lab, acting as a state witness, indicated that shortening the barrel of the 20-gauge shotgun likely had no effect or "negligible" effect at close range.)

Smith went to his daughter's bedrooms and watched them sleep. He wrote good-bye letters to each of them. The note to 12-year-old Colleen, his oldest, said:

"My sweetheart! You are my sargent (sic); and I always count on you! I have tried so hard and nothing seems to work out. I am so sorry that I could not do a better job. Colleen, always look after your sisters for me; keep them together with you and protect them. I know it will not be easy, but you are smart and strong.

"I am so proud of you, you made every day wonderful for your dad! For almost 13 years my Arizona baby has worked so hard to be a good girl. I love you so much. Help Tammy please; she wants to be like you so much.

"Thank you Colleen, Love Dad.

p.s. 'Drive and shoot; Drive and shoot.' "

(This last was basketball advice.)

He gathered up his pack and guns, a hunting rifle and a large handgun, and a hunting knife, got behind the wheel of his 1991 maroon Ford Ranger 4x4 pickup, headed north on Brisky Canyon Road for a few hundred yards in the chilly and rainy darkness, turned right on Brender Canyon Road, down the road about four miles past pear and apple orchards into Cashmere.

"I knew that when I went down the road that basically this was–it was like being at war–like this was it; that I never would be back; I mean it was a terrible feeling."

He parked behind his ex-wife's house, 215 Washington Street, which was a residential street a block south of the Burlington Northern tracks. The house was dark. His ex-wife was alone, asleep in her bedroom. Her new husband was away at his job in the Tri-Cities, 135 miles away.

Arnold: "Did you have your knife with you."

"Yes, I did."

"It was crystal clear. I mean, I was just resolved to it. It wasn't because I was mad or angry. You know, I had tears and everything, but there was no way out … . Tomorrow just couldn't come for my kids in the same way."

"And so did you go into Ann Smith Patrick's house with your knife?"

"Yeah. I ran right down the back and, you know, tried not to even–tried to disassociate, you know, my feelings or my thinking, and ran right through the back door. I didn't even know the layout of the house. I had never been to her house. I knew it was just a little old wooden shacky place. And I ran right in there. There were no lights; it was all dark. I had a flashlight … I was frightened by the situation and didn't want to know–didn't want to see nothing … . I wasn't trained or knew what I was doing, really, and I was frightened by the whole thing."

"Did you use the knife on Ann?"

"Yeah."

Arnold asked Smith why he hadn't used one of the guns instead of a knife. Smith had brought a .357-caliber Magnum revolver, a .308-caliber lever-action hunting rifle and the 20-gauge shotgun with him in the pickup.

"Well, I didn't give it a great deal of thought. All I knew is that I wanted everything to happen very fast and as painless as I thought it could be. And I knew–I had been a meat cutter, and I had helped my dad in the slaughter business … and I knew the knife was quick and fast. And I was familiar with using a knife … . I wasn't there to torture or terrorize anybody. I just wanted it over with, and I wanted it as easy as possible. So I just thought of using the knife."

In this portion of his testimony, Smith gave no further details of stabbing his ex-wife to death.

In a subsequent court document, Smith said the time between leaving his pickup and returning to it was six minutes.

"Where did you go when you left the house?"

Smith said he drove up the hill, a long block, to Hovda's house, parked and grabbed the shotgun. "Why did you use the shotgun?" Arnold asked.

Smith replied he assumed the single-shot 20-gauge with the barrel shortened was like "a low-powered pistol," especially when loaded with birdshot (small pellets). He smashed through a side door, "stumbled up the stairs," and didn't know what to expect because he did not know the layout of the two-story house. "So it surprised me that she was standing right there, and I pushed her back in the room."

"She came forward, and I shot. And she kept coming forward. I took my gun, just kind of a reflex thing like that, and I thought I hit her across the shoulders and hit her on the head because I was frightened that she was coming for me. She was reaching for me, trying to grab for me, and so I was able to side step and run out of the house."

"Did you intend to kill her?"

"No."

Smith said if he had intended to kill her, he would have used either the .357 pistol or the hunting knife. He was carrying both in the deep pockets of the heavy long dark coat he was wearing. In a convoluted way, he tried to explain that he wanted her to live so that she would have to answer people who wondered why she had interfered in his children's lives. The same went for the LaVignes, his next stop. "Why couldn't they leave them alone?"

The LaVignes lived in a one-story house on a steep hill above Cashmere High School about a mile from the Hovda residence.

"Bill, did you then go to the LaVignes?"

"Yes."

"Did you shoot them?"

"Yes."

"Did you intend to kill them?"

"No, I didn't."

Smith said he had known Duane LaVigne for years. In fact, Duane once was his insurance man, "and I couldn't fathom why for years and years him and his wife were in the middle of all this stuff … taking such a disregard for the lives of my kids."

Smith's most specific complaint was that Margaret, his youngest child, was visiting the LaVigne's cabin at Lake Wenatchee and fell off a dock and almost drowned. He blamed the LaVignes for not being more careful. He also didn't like some of the houses the LaVignes had rented to his ex-wife. When pressed by Arnold about why he didn't intend to kill them, Smith said, "Well, they were old … they just were well-intending people, but they just didn't realize the problems or how bad things were."

He gave up on his explaining and briefly told what he had done that early morning, Friday, March 6, described by Smith as "rainy, cold and windy."

"I had walked in there, and Duane stood up, and I had my shotgun up … I just kind of froze there … I was kind of chanting a thing to myself, and I froze. And then Duane yelled at me or said something to me, and I just shot him. And I just popped it open, put another shell in.

"And I saw Jane LaVigne pulling blankets up to protect herself, so I waited until she got the blankets all up to protect herself, and I thought I shot her in the ribs. I didn't really think that it was–that the shotgun shell or that birdshot would going to even really do more than maybe break the skin … . I just turned around and walked out. I wasn't thinking about, you know, I wasn't thinking about nothing."

Pressed by Arnold for more detail on the chanting to himself, the effort to disconnect, Smith said he was "trying to keep himself strong enough to do these things … None of it was good, none of it was making me happy … . I was there on business."

Asked if the acts of the night were right, Smith answered, "Yes. Oh, yeah, sure. Yes."

"Bill, let me ask you one more question. Do you think you are a dangerous person?"

"No, I'm not dangerous."

He viewed what he had done as something any father who really loved their children would do. "When kids need your help … you perceive yourself as their shield, as their person who has to be there for them."

"Okay, Bill. Thank you. No further questions."

Prosecutor Riesen stood to cross-examine.

The prosecutor bored in quickly to try to establish that Smith was familiar with firearms. He asked him about his Air Force service and wondered if it had included weapons training. He likely was disappointed with the answer. Smith told him the Air Force basic training, in his case, included one day of rifle practice, which boiled down to shooting a rifle once. "One shot."

Asked if he had hunted as a child, Smith said he had, with his father, but never owned a shotgun until 1970 or so. "The shotgun here?" Riesen asked, pointing to the inexpensive FIE Brazilian-made shotgun used in shooting Mrs. Hovda and the LaVignes.

"Yes."

Persistent questioning showed that Smith did shoot birds occasionally, but also indicated he was not much of a marksman and apparently had no good idea what a 20-gauge shotgun would do at close range. Smith did agree the shotgun in question probably would kill somebody if fired while being held against a person's head.

(Riesen was incredulous when Smith said he did not intend to kill Ms. Hovda or the LaVignes even though he shot them at close range. Anyone who has fired a 20-gauge shotgun point-blank at a close target will sympathize with the prosecutor's skepticism. I tried it, firing 20-gauge No. 8 birdshot at a plastic target a few feet away. The result was a hole almost four inches in diameter.)

Further questioning indicated Smith had brought his .308 hunting rifle, equipped with a telescopic sight, so he would be able "to scope things out."

Riesen asked if this comment meant shooting somebody at a longer distance.

Smith replied he wanted to identify people through the scope, and one of his thoughts had been he wanted to find Judge John E. Bridges to ask him some questions about what had happened in his court during the divorce and child custody fight.

"So you thought you would ask him by shooting him through the scope?"

Smith denied that, but did say he was "at war" and considered that Judge Bridges "had done a lot of things that I didn't understand that were crooked and criminal. There had been no appearance of him following the law or anything like that, and I wanted to tell him why it was all so important."

Smith also denied that killing his ex-wife was against the law. Riesen didn't pursue the denial, possibly because he didn't want to buttress the defense case that Smith was delusional. Later, Smith agreed he was surprised he was on trial for murder because he assumed he would be killed, not arrested.

Asked if he were shocked that he was charged with murdering his ex-wife, Smith said he was shocked. "That's a shock to you?" Riesen repeated.

"Yes."

"You have a lot of other friends of yours that have killed their ex-wives and not gotten charged with murder?"

Smith's answer, to this somewhat sarcastic question, was based, he said, on seven months of thinking while behind bars: "You know, I have to tell you I don't think of it as the word 'murder.' I don't think it is murder … . What I thought was, it was something I had to do."

Smith, in response to more of Riesen's questions, said the thought of going to jail for two days to serve his sentence for contempt of court, didn't bother him at all. "That was no sweat … . I had taunted the judges for years to send me to jail."

Regarding the stabbing death of his ex-wife, Smith said "in a lot of ways both her and I was going to be at peace so that, you know, I didn't see this necessarily as a terrible, bad thing."

Asked if he had "emotional feelings" while killing his ex-wife, Smith said he didn't know. He was not mad or angry. "I always felt sorry for her. I married her because I felt sorry for her. I never did love her; I told her that. The day we got married I told her. The worst day of my life probably was the day I left England and left her there. I felt bad for her. She was crying, and she wanted so bad–she told me she wanted to get married. I always felt sorry for her."

In his testimony, Smith also said, besides Judge Bridges, he was looking for two lawyers, Chancey Crowell, who had represented his wife, and Steve Richardson, court appointed to represent his children. His emphasis, however, seemed to be on Judge Bridges.

At the end of his cross-examination, Riesen asked Smith if he thought anything was wrong with him at that moment.

"No, I don't think there is anything wrong with me."

"Why did you file an insanity plea in this case?"

Smith replied, "You're paying this guy (meaning Arnold). He's not my lawyer. You're paying him. He's the one running my defense. You're paying him, not me."

"So, you never asked him to file an insanity defense for you?"

"I'm not insane. I'm not crazy. I'll tell you that right now."

"You knew exactly what you were doing the night you did all of these things, didn't you?"

"I knew, I knew what I was doing," Smith said.

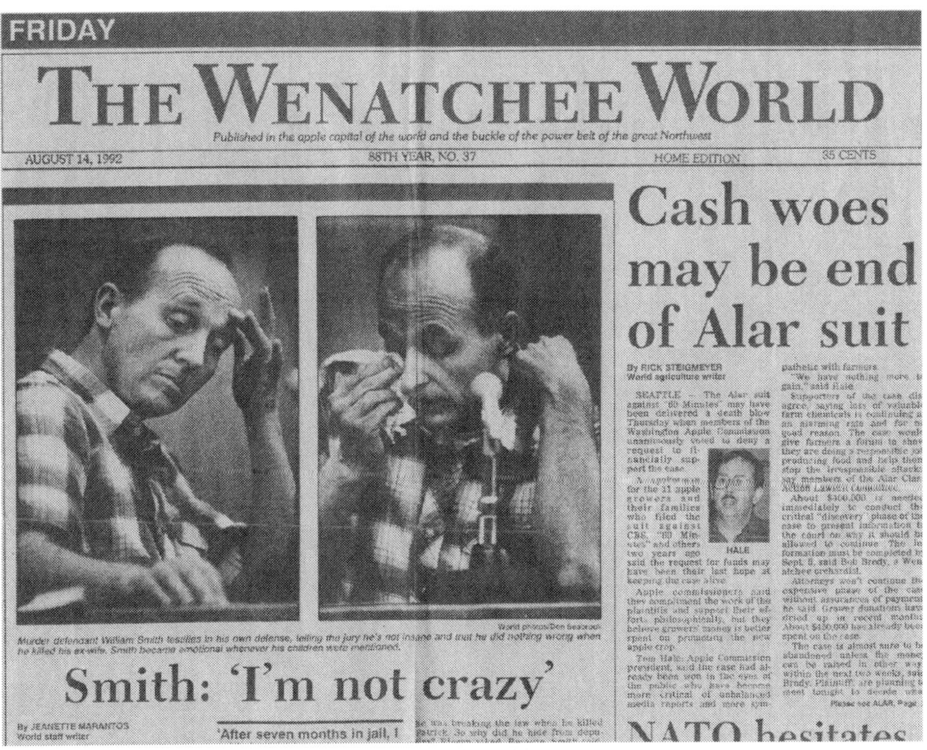

FRIDAY

THE WENATCHEE WORLD

Published in the apple capital of the world and the buckle of the power belt of the great Northwest

AUGUST 14, 1992 | 88TH YEAR, NO. 37 | HOME EDITION | 35 CENTS

Cash woes may be end of Alar suit

By RICK STEIGMEYER
World agriculture writer

SEATTLE — The Alar suit against "60 Minutes" may have been delivered a death blow Thursday when members of the Washington Apple Commission unanimously voted to deny a request to financially support the case.

HALE

Please see ALAR, Page

Murder defendant William Smith testifies in his own defense, telling the jury he's not insane and that he did nothing wrong when he killed his ex-wife. Smith became emotional whenever his children were mentioned.

Smith: 'I'm not crazy'

By JEANETTE MARANTOS
World staff writer

'After seven months in jail, I

NATO hesitates

Bill Smith on the witness stand. Photos by Don Seabrook.

In his opening statement, Arnold had predicted his client would deny he was insane and Smith had just proved him right. Even so, it must have seemed like an opening for the prosecution in its effort to discount Smith's insanity plea. The subject came up the next day for clarification, but for the moment was not pursued by either side.

Riesen turned to the judge and told her, "That's all the questions I have."

Arnold, on redirect examination, asked Smith if he had wanted to kill anyone with a gun, would he have used the hunting rifle? "Sure," said Smith. "No more questions," said Arnold.

"Nothing further," said Riesen.

"All right, Mr. Smith, you may step down," the judge told him.

Chapter 4
Testimony

Bill Smith during his time on the witness stand was calm and brief when describing what he had done. Elaboration and feeling were lacking, except when explaining, sometimes in tears, why he was anguished about his children. His description of the crimes was sketchy, almost bare of details. This skeletal approach to a series of violent events was vastly different from the testimony of other witnesses, including the county coroner, the three surviving victims, and the emergency room physicians.

For law enforcement, the violent night began at 12:11 a.m. March 6, when the emergency dispatcher got a call from Rebecca Hovda's daughter to say her mother had been shot. Deputy Sheriff Randy Foltz responded to the Hovda address, 112 Chase St., a two-story brick house in an upscale Cashmere neighborhood. On the witness stand, Deputy Foltz said when he arrived he noticed that a side door was open and the frame had been splintered. Mrs. Hovda's 13-year-old daughter was sitting on the stairs. She took the deputy to her mother's bedroom, where Mrs. Hovda was lying on the bloody bed. She was not able to speak, Foltz said. The emergency aid unit arrived at about that time.

Foltz heard Duane LaVigne's voice calling for help on his radio's fire department frequency. A friend of Mrs. Hovda, Bev Mack (who later married Robert Patrick, Ann Smith Patrick's widowed husband), arrived and the deputy asked her if she knew of anyone who might be a common enemy of Mrs. Hovda and Duane LaVigne. "Bev Mack told me that Becky (Hovda) was a friend of Ann Smith, and I knew that Ann Smith was a friend of the LaVignes." Ms. Mack told Deputy Foltz a possible suspect would be Bill Smith.

Foltz radioed his office and asked that an officer be sent to Ann Smith Patrick's house, just down the hill at 215 Washington St. Deputies who responded quickly said there was a yellow Ford sedan in the driveway and the rear door of the house had been forced. A woman was found apparently lifeless in bed in the street side bedroom. She was covered in blankets. A closer examination showed "a large gaping" wound in her neck, with a great deal of blood on the blankets, sheets, the wall above the bed and the carpet. Her body "was warm to the touch." Deputies quickly searched the house. The kitchen was neat with clean dishes in a rack. A porcelain teapot was in the sink. Coroner Gerald Rappe was called, but he waited until the sheriff's office investigators had finished. Rappe, a medical doctor and pathologist, began his work at about 2:30 a.m. on March 6.

Judge Wardell warned courtroom spectators that the coming testimony from the coroner would "not be pleasant and they should leave now if they couldn't handle it."

During his testimony and in the autopsy report Rappe said that his first impression was "a large amount of blood," so much blood the victim's blue nightie and a blue blanket were soaked in red. His "significant findings" were multiple penetrating stab wounds to the neck, chest, right shoulder and right upper back, at least eight separate wounds. The blade would have been about five inches long and five-eighths of an inch wide, pointed and likely double bladed. There was no evidence of other injuries, and the only sign of physical defect detected during the autopsy was a mild gall bladder inflammation.

Bill Smith's Buck hunting knife in evidence was consistent with all characteristics of the death weapon, Rappe testified.

During his testimony, the coroner stood a few feet from Bill Smith, who remained impassive. His only movement was moving his chair from side to side. As his attorney studied the autopsy photos, Smith remained expressionless.

A dispute between the attorneys developed over introducing the autopsy photos as evidence. Defense attorney Dan Arnold argued they would "inflame" the jury because of their "gruesome nature." Prosecutor Gary Riesen countered that the photos were relevant to the crime, and the prosecution's role was not "to sanitize the crime of murder." Judge Carol Wardell agreed with Riesen. "A bloody crime cannot be explained to the jury in a lily white manner," the judge said.

The victim likely was asleep on her stomach when she was stabbed twice with great force in the right side of her upper back, the coroner said. She came around to face her attacker from the right, was stabbed on the back of her right hand, then on the front of the same hand, the front of the left hand and on the left arm. Her hands were injured seriously, with one finger almost severed.

"There was a brief, but furious battle in which legs were used. There is smeared blood on the legs, smeared blood even on the bottom of her feet to indicate the legs were used in a furious battle. But, as she was turning, the stabbing was going on." Rappe described a series of wounds in the neck that sliced her Adam's apple and her vocal cords.

"And then at least one stab wound severed the carotid artery and the internal jugular vein on the right ... . At the time that they were severed, you get this furious activity which gets the blood pressure up, and the bleeding would have been extremely rapid, and she would have been unconscious, hypotensive and near death within a minute.

Time of death was sometime between 10 p.m. March 5 and 12:30 a.m. March 6.

The coroner's finding: Death by homicide.

During my initial research, I spent some time in Prosecutor Riesen's office reading his voluminous file on the Smith case. "Knife killings are always vicious," Riesen told me, and showed me with his hands his idea of the stabbing movements and how he imagined Bill Smith had cut Ann's throat. "Stab, stab, stab, very gory, awful."

Riesen's office was on a corner of the fifth floor of the courthouse, with a view of snowy hills and mountains beyond. "They gave me a good view," he said. "It helps makes up for the unpleasant aspects of the job."

Years later, in 2012 after Riesen had been county prosecutor for 27 years, I was in touch with him again with some questions. "This is a case," he said, "I will never get out of my head–I can still see the brutality of the crime scene in his ex-wife's home. The miracle is that no one else died that night or in the following days."

Among the prosecution's first witnesses were Rebecca Hovda and Duane and Jane LaVigne. Their accounts of the early morning of March 6 were like nightmares I assume many people have had, specifically the horror of being awakened in the dark of night by a man with a gun who clearly intended to do you great harm.

Rebecca Hovda, 44, was the first victim to testify. She had only recently been released from home health care and still was not fully recovered from her very extensive shotgun injuries. She testified she had gone to bed in her second floor bedroom between 11 and midnight the night of March 5, and was alone in the house except for two daughters, aged 7 and 13. Her husband was away on business. She was awakened out of a sound sleep by a crashing sound, which she thought might have been the family dog knocking something over. She got out of bed, opened her bedroom door and had stepped into the unlighted hall when she saw a man at the head of the stairs. He was dressed in a long dark coat and was wearing a hat.

"He–he came forward, and I can't tell you whether he actually pushed me into the bedroom or whether I was backing up. I believe I said something very intelligent like, 'What is going on out here?' He never spoke."

The next thing she remembered was a gun being pushed into her stomach, "and I recognized who it was."

"Who was it?" Riesen asked.

"Bill Smith."

"He pulled the trigger, and I remember my thought (was) I couldn't understand why I wasn't waking up from my bad dream. I put my hands over my stomach, and I remember looking down toward my stomach, and that's when I saw the butt end of the gun coming up toward my head out of the corner of my eye. And that's basically the last thing I remember until when I came to … I must have blacked out because when I came to, I was on the bed. I was standing when he hit me. But I heard his footsteps retreating, and I heard my daughter, Maija, getting up out of bed."

Hovda told Riesen the expression on Bill Smith's face when he shot her was "very determined, very purposeful." It was not "a wild look," she said.

Earlier in her testimony, Hovda described her close friendship with Ann Smith and her support for her friend during the divorce and custody disputes. She said she had little contact with Bill Smith during the divorce process, although she was aware he was not happy with her strong backing of Ann Smith.

During cross-examination by Dan Arnold, Hovda repeated she had given "moral" support to Ann Smith. She said she and Bill Smith had never exchanged "harsh words" and had never had an argument.

The state called Duane LaVigne, who was 65 in 1992. His wife, Jane, testified immediately after her husband. The LaVignes lived about a mile from Ms. Hovda, up the hill from the high school. LaVigne, who had lived in Cashmere since 1953, operated an insurance firm and he and his wife owned rental property, including the house where Ann Smith Patrick had been slain. They knew Ann through their church, Cashmere United Methodist. LaVigne did not testify during the Smith divorce and child custody fight. His wife did. He and his wife had been supporters of Ann for some time, including giving her and her children a place to stay. LaVigne was best man when Ann Smith married Bob Patrick in February 1992, not long before she was killed.

LaVigne was acquainted with Bill Smith and had been a friend for years with Bill's father, Bob, who also was a Cashmere insurance man. LaVigne had sold insurance to Bill Smith during his Air Force service.

Riesen asked LaVigne to describe what happened at 402 Valley View Drive in the very early morning of March 6.

"Well, as you heard, I'm a volunteer on the fire department, and I was awakened by a call about a gunshot wound on Chase Street. I laid there for a minute. I do not normally respond on emergency medical calls. I assist when I can. On this particular case, I thought perhaps I would.

"I got up and turned the bedside light on and picked up the phone book to look up another address on Chase Street to give me a bearing on what side of the street it might be occurring. It was at that time I heard a sound in our home, and then the bedroom door slammed open. And I was sitting on the edge of the bed. This gentleman or this person came in, was wearing a black coat and a black hat. It happened so quickly that I did not recognize nor know what was taking place until a gun was raised up from out of the coat, and the only thing I saw at that moment was the shiny end of a barrel. And that's when I knew I was in trouble.

"The gun was fired. I saw the flame and felt the heat and the shot. I fell to the floor and let out a gasp of air, hoping that whoever it was that was shooting me would not shoot again. It was a very deliberate procedure up to that time, and I thought maybe that was it. I laid still.

"Next thing I heard, of course, was I heard my wife say something. The next I heard was a shot. It wasn't meant for me; I knew it was Jane. We both lied very silent. I didn't actually hear the person leave, but it was very silent. And as I recall, I said a little prayer … ."

LaVigne said he managed to call for help on his two-way radio. "Fortunately–it was through no fault of the assailant's shooting that we didn't die on the spot; it was the fact that my fellow firemen and EMT members were already en route to the first incident," and they alerted the private ambulance firm as well. He said those factors saved their lives along with the Ballard Ambulance crew and the skills of the doctors and nurses at the hospital in Wenatchee.

"From that point on a lot of it kind of escapes me. I'm in and out of it."

Riesen asked LaVigne to stand and show the jury where he was shot. LaVigne did so and pointed to his abdomen, saying the shotgun blast took part of his colon, his appendix and damaged his hipbone. LaVigne demonstrated how he was sitting on the edge of the bed with the phone book in his lap, turned to the letter M. LaVigne said he began to get up when the man entered the room. LaVigne thought he said, "What is going on here?" There was no reply.

The shotgun was fired from about six feet away, through the telephone book and into LaVigne's side. Investigators later said the bedroom was full of confetti from the shotgun-shredded telephone book. LaVigne said the sequence took no more than a minute or two. He did not hear the man reload the single-shot 20-gauge shotgun. LaVigne said he heard the second shot, then it was silent until he called for help on his radio.

Arnold, during his cross-examination, asked LaVigne if he and Bill Smith had ever exchanged harsh words or had an argument during the legal disputes with Ann Smith. "No, no harsh words. Maybe some disparaging stares and maybe something of that nature, but that would be my opinion; it may not have been his intent."

On redirect, Riesen asked for more elaboration on what LaVigne saw of the shooter, if he got a good look at his face. "Well, to be very honest," LaVigne said, "what I recall was a smile just prior to shooting, and a little mustache, or at least I gave a description of the individual, in fact, over the radio and I called it a Charlie Chaplin. I don't know whether it had been darkened or whether it was a mustache or what it was, but that's what I saw."

"You recall a smile" Riesen asked.

"And a little smirk."

The state next called Jane LaVigne.

Ms. LaVigne, 62, a slim woman, took the stand. During her testimony, she said 53 shotgun pellets remained in her neck and lungs, some of them too close to her spinal cord to be removed safely. The prosecutor established that Ms. LaVigne had met Ann Smith at her church, United Methodist. They became friends while working on various projects together, including Ann's English high teas, Sunday school and choir practice. Ms. LaVigne said after they became friends, she and her husband opened their home to Ann and their children during and after the divorce, and also provided hospitality at their cabin on Lake Wenatchee.

In addition, Ms. LaVigne said she had written an affidavit regarding a "derogatory" telephone call to her from Bill Smith. She had testified in court during the child custody dispute about the angry call, during which she said Bill Smith had called her "a good Christian woman that was supporting a murderer." She said she did not think he was referring to the abortion obtained by Ann Smith, but rather her support for Ann and helping with the children. In her testimony during the custody hearing, she said she had never seen Bill Smith mistreat his children.

After dealing with these incidentals, Riesen got to the main point and asked Ms. LaVigne to describe the events of March 6.

"I was in a deep sleep, and then I was aware that Duane had turned on the light and was sitting on the edge of the bed. I hadn't clearly heard what had come over the radio. I wasn't aware there had been a shooting. I heard our front door open and the steps coming into the house. And the door to the bedroom like it had been kicked open. And a man coming into our room dressed in dark clothes and a dark overcoat. I didn't see his face at that time.

"I saw the fire from the gun. I heard my husband cry out and fall to the floor. I was so terrorized and so frightened that I screamed; and as he turned towards me and I looked directly into his face with the bedroom light on. I recognized Bill Smith."

"The same Bill Smith that is here in court today?" Riesen asked.

"Yes."

"There is no doubt in your mind that's who it was?"

"There is no doubt."

She continued. "I was laying in bed. I must have been almost halfway sitting up. And I said something like 'No, no, please no.' " And I saw the shotgun come up, and in that last instant I flung myself back and snatched at the comforter off the bed, and I felt the blast of the shot in my neck. And it was quiet. And still. And I believed we were left for dead.

"I thought he was still in the house, and when I heard Duane's voice, I said to Duane, 'He's still here.' And Duane said to me, 'No, it's all right, honey. He's gone. He's gone.' And I heard Duane make the call to the aid car. I heard him say to the men, 'Come quickly. I don't think we're going to make it.' I thought we were going to die.

"I heard my husband begin to cry out in pain. Thinking that I would die, I wanted to assure him of my love. I told my husband of my love for him. We began to pray aloud, 'Dear God, help us. Dear God, help us.' And then I don't have any memory for two or three days."

The man who shot them, she said, was silent throughout.

Ms. LaVigne's wounds were in her neck and upper-right chest, with serious damage to her vocal cords. Part of her right breast was shot away.

In other testimony, two of the physicians at Central Washington Hospital in Wenatchee who worked on the three victims said all were lucky to be alive. All were critical when they arrived, and three of the regional hospital's operating rooms were immediately placed in service.

Dr. Mark Shipman said Ms. Hovda had no blood pressure and was near death when the paramedics reached her. Her abdominal and intestinal injuries "were massive." She had a hole the size of a grapefruit in her stomach wall, resulting in the removal of her spleen, most of her pancreas and most of her stomach.

He said Ms. Hovda was not expected to survive.

Shipman said Duane LaVigne was alert when he came into the hospital, with an acute shotgun wound to the upper abdomen and perforated intestines, life-threatening wounds. "Without rapid medical help, neither Ms. Hovda nor Mr. LaVigne would have survived."

Dr. Timothy Patton, a specialist in head and neck surgery, treated Jane LaVigne. Her neck wound had caused breathing difficulty so severe he performed an emergency tracheotomy in the operating room and placed a breathing tube in her airway. Otherwise, she would have died in a minute or two or suffered major brain damage.

Another wound was perilously close, about one-fourth inch, from her right internal jugular vein and carotid artery. If these had been cut by the shotgun blast, she would have bled to death in a minute, Patton said. The birdshot had penetrated her upper chest on the right side, resulting in "a sucking chest wound" because of air leaking through the chest wall.

"It's a miracle this woman lived, yes," Patton said.

After leaving the LaVigne's hilltop house, Smith paused in a nearby driveway across from the Cashmere Middle School while the emergency vehicles sped past, then proceeded down Pioneer Avenue and turned south on Mission Creek Road, heading into a mountainous, sparsely populated area. Years later, during a prison interview, Smith said he abandoned his pickup "in an overwrought and edgy state" and left some things behind, including a list of judges, lawyers and others. A list of three names was included in the inventory of items found on Smith or in his pack when arrested, but this list was not included in trial evidence.

(As an aside, Smith also has maintained that he left at his residence a detailed journal of his dispute with Ann Smith. This journal has never been mentioned officially in detail, except for a brief notation in a sheriff's report of a diary or journal being found on a kitchen table at Smith's residence. No one remembers seeing it or reading it. Smith insisted that in the journal he explained what he was doing, and why.)

The manhunt was a tense time for the Cashmere and Wenatchee area. Lawyers and judges, as well as ordinary citizens who had had problems with Smith, were warned by police and sheriff's deputies they might be in danger. Hardware stores reported a record business in guns and ammunition. Smith was armed and clearly dangerous. It was not clear if he would have killed again, but few wanted to take a chance. People started locking their doors. Many slept with loaded shotguns next to their bed.

Chancey Crowell, one of Ann Smith's attorneys, and a target of Bill Smith's intense dislike, got the warning call at 3 a.m. Friday, less than three hours after the crimes. His first reaction was to load his gun. His second reaction, he told *The Wenatchee World,* was to gather his wife and children, close his office and leave town for the weekend. Child and family counselor Vicki Bones and her husband woke her children and they all went to an all-night café and later waited at a friend's house for Smith to be arrested. Sharen Fisher, a woman particularly despised by Smith, was a former director of Wenatchee's rape crisis clinic and one of Ann Smith's counselors. She told the newspaper that she took her warning call seriously and asked the mayor to assign a police officer to her house immediately. (Smith was carrying her address with him when arrested. Another address belonged to Judge John Bridges.) Attorney Steve Richardson, yet another name on Smith's mental list of despised people, jumped out of bed after the 4 a.m. call, and he and his wife packed their children into their car and spent the rest of the night in a hotel. "No clothes, no shoes" for the children, his wife said.

One Cashmere woman, a friend of Ann Smith who had testified in support of Ann at several court hearings, went into hiding after her name was heard on the police scanner as one of the persons possibly threatened by Smith. Long after he was caught, she said she was still terrified of him. She refused to testify at any court hearing unless Smith was in handcuffs and leg irons.

Chelan County residents, at least some of them, were right in not taking any chances. Kevin T. Kelly, a supervisor on the adult psychiatric unit at Eastern State Hospital, where Smith eventually was committed for a few days of mental evaluation, testified that Smith told mental health workers that he had gone "hunting judges and lawyers that night" and his "only mistake was not doing it sooner." Smith described himself "as an eternal warrior." He was "glad he did it and he would do it again if he had to," Kelly testified.

Undersheriff Pat Beatie, a former FBI agent, was in command of the search. He testified that Smith's Ford Ranger pickup was spotted Friday morning on a mountain road off Mission Creek Road 12 miles south of Cashmere. A nearby cabin had been broken into, presumably by Smith. A person was sighted on a ridgeline toward evening and the area was "saturated" by officers, who by this time included Chelan County deputies, Wenatchee police, and members of the Washington State Patrol. Shortly after the first sighting on the ridge, a man was seen running on another ridge as darkness was falling. Looking for an armed and suspected killer in the dark was deemed too dangerous, so the active search was called off for the night.

During the night of March 6, some 250 fliers identifying Bill Smith as the wanted man and a photo of him were circulated in the area. Judge John Bridges, who lived in the general area of Squilchuck and Halvorson canyons where the search was most intense had been warned that he possibly was in danger. "Some people were so fearful that we actually had them taken to secure locations. Judge Bridges was among these people," Beatie said.

The active search resumed at dawn on Saturday, March 7, a fair and warm day. The break came when Joe Halliday, 41, returned to his Halvorson Canyon house south of Wenatchee a little after 8 a.m. after working the night shift at Keyes Fibre. He saw that his house had been broken into, but a quick search showed nothing missing. He noticed that his washer and dryer had been used. Then he spotted Smith behind a bedroom door. Halliday recognized him from the wanted flier. Before Halliday fled, he heard Smith say, "Hey, wait, I won't hurt you. I just needed a place to spend the night." Halliday didn't wait to pursue the conversation.

Deputies arrived quickly. They did not find Bill Smith, but they did find 40 marijuana plants growing inside Halliday's house. In an ironic twist, Halliday's call to the sheriff's office to report a man wanted for murder cost him a bundle. He was charged with a felony for growing marijuana. He pleaded guilty and wound up being fined $1,000, and contributing $2,500 to a drug task force as part of a sentencing agreement. In all, his good citizenship, with attorney's fees and court costs included, probably set him back more than $4,000. Halliday was cooperative throughout and even sent Christmas cards to the prosecutor who had handled his case.

After the Halliday call, Beatie said the helicopter was dispatched and officers, including the county's SWAT team, poured into the sparsely-populated rural neighborhood. Beatie said he was certain Smith had not escaped the dragnet and was hiding in the heavy brush and rough terrain of the immediate vicinity. He decided Smith had fled into a canyon, more like a deep gully filled with heavy brush and poison ivy, behind the Halliday house. Late in the afternoon, some 30 officers did a straight line search, with the men about 10 feet apart. Beatie was close to two officers, both SWAT members carrying submachine guns. One of them shouted, "I have a pack!" and pointed his gun toward what he had seen.

Beatie looked closer and could see a man under a blue coat, breathing heavily and curled on his left side into a fetal position, not moving. "Don't move or I'll shoot. Don't move or I'll shoot. Don't move or I'll kill you!" Beatie pointed his 9mm pistol at Smith. A lever-action rifle with a telescopic sight was leaning against a large bush a foot away from Smith.

Beatie pulled the coat off and told Smith "not to move, not to breathe," or he would shoot. Smith said, "I'm not moving." Another officer handcuffed him.

"He was very clearly afraid and very rationally in control of himself so as not to get shot," Beatie said. Beatie asked a Wenatchee police captain to read Smith his rights and to be absolutely certain his rights were read to him. "At that point, I heard the subject say that he wanted to see an attorney. Those were the only other words I heard him utter."

MONDAY

THE WENATCHEE WORLD

Published in the apple capital of the world and the buckle of the power belt of the great Northwest

MARCH 9, 1992 | 87TH YEAR, NO. 214 | HOME EDITION | 35 CENTS

Murder suspect captured

Smith was still stalking enemies, officers say

By MICHELLE PARTRIDGE
World staff writer

WENATCHEE — Law offic-

... Smith was arrested on one count of first-degree murder and three counts of attempted ...

Harkin drops out of race

WASHINGTON (AP) — Iowa Sen. Tom Harkin, who cast himself as the liberal heir to Democratic presidents of the past, quit the 1992 race today after a string of poor showings and said he would "pay any price" to help defeat President Bush.

"Circumstances may change, but the work of care and compassion still continues," Harkin told an audience at Gallaudet University, a school for the deaf. He signed the beginning of his remarks to his audience before stepping to the microphone.

HARKIN

Harkin's departure came four days after a similar withdrawal statement by Sen. Bob Kerrey of Nebraska. The remaining Democrats — Bill Clinton, Paul Tsongas and Jerry Brown — were pointing toward an 11-state showdown on Tuesday.

Harkin's withdrawal was rife with symbolism.

His brother Frank is deaf, and the selection of Gallaudet was meant to underscore a campaign commitment to Americans with disabilities.

The man who depicted himself as heir to Franklin Roosevelt and John Kennedy wryly paraphrased JFK as he dropped out, and kidded his remaining rivals at the same time:

"I will pay any price, bear any ...

Bill Smith, with Detective Daryl Mathena. Photo by Tom Williams.

Besides the .308-caliber lever action rifle, Smith also had a .357-caliber Magnum Dan Wesson revolver and the Brazilian-made 20-gauge single-shot shotgun. All were loaded. Inside the pack, officers found what turned out to be the murder knife in a black leather sheath, its blade covered with blood. Also found were maps of Chelan County and Wenatchee and East Wenatchee; notes, with addresses of several judges and attorneys, including 2210 Hampton Road, Judge Bridges' address, which was in the vicinity where Smith was arrested. More prosaic items, too, including toilet paper, crackers, a flashlight and matches. Smith was wearing his blue postal worker pants and a blue shirt.

Defense attorney Arnold asked Beatie if he really meant it when he said he would shoot Smith if he breathed. "I assume that was hyperbole just to get his attention. You wouldn't have shot him if he breathed?"

"I wouldn't describe it as hyperbole," Beatie said. "I would describe it as the intent to take psychological control of the situation."

During one of my conversations with Smith around a Formica-topped table, the type seemingly always present in prison visiting rooms, he remembered "a tall, skinny black state patrolman" named John R. Batiste. He said Batiste stepped in front of him and probably saved his life during the capture. "I assumed I would be killed," Smith said. Two of the deputies, whom Smith described as nervous and trigger-happy, had submachine guns and likely would have fired if Batiste had not shielded him, he said. Smith also credited Batiste with immediately telling him he should ask for a lawyer.

I called Batiste at his office in Olympia, Washington, to ask him for his recollections of that day. Batiste became the chief of the Washington State Patrol in 2005.

"I was a lieutenant in Wenatchee in 1992 and taking part in the manhunt," Batiste told me. "Smith was hiding in tall grass, sort of burrowed in. I was very close to him when he moved. I almost stepped on him. He was ordered out, with his hands up. I was focused on him, on no one else. I don't remember shielding him. I may have read him his Miranda warning. I do remember that everyone there was relieved he was in custody without incident."

Batiste said Smith was viewed as "a very dangerous man who had committed terrible crimes. It would be interesting to know what went on in his mind."

Smith also has repeated his belief that people were taken into protective custody, possibly by the state patrol, during the manhunt. He thought Batiste might know something about it. I asked Batiste, who said he did not know, but assumed the sheriff's office would. It is true that some people, including Judge Bridges, were offered protection by the sheriff's office in a secure location. Not everybody took advantage of the offer.

Smith was taken to the Chelan County sheriff's office. He was interviewed at length by Detective Daryl Mathena with Sgt. C.T. Winn, Jr. also present. In his report, which was included in the prosecutor's file, Mathena said Smith was talkative, in fact talked steadily and "obsessively" about his concern "for the well being" of his daughters. With no prompting, Mathena said Smith talked about the divorce, and the "constant court battles, lawyers, judges, his ex-wife, all sucking him dry."

He complained that Judge Bridges laughed at him in court and threw his paperwork into the garbage without reading it, and was sure Judge Small had done the same. Smith was emotional, angry to the point of tears, Mathena said. No one would listen to him. Attorneys and land developers were trying to steal his land for development and his ex-wife was part of it. People accused him of "programming" his kids.

"The last three days were the most peaceful of the past four years," Smith told the detective.

He agreed he had been advised of his rights and was willing to talk. He felt no remorse. At least this way, he said, he could see his kids once in a while and would no longer worry that his ex-wife was abusing them.

He told Mathena he could have shot police officers during the search and could have shot at the helicopter. He had no intention of "putting a gun barrel in his mouth." He had spent the last couple of days mostly sleeping and "being peaceful with no worries."

He denied knowing anything about shooting Ms. Hovda and the LaVignes. When asked about killing Ann Smith, he replied, "I don't know anything about that." He rambled on about counselors and became angry when interrupted. Smith said Ann Smith's new husband was "a nice guy" although he had a couple of kids who said mean and cruel things to his girls. He was afraid his ex-wife would get custody of his daughters and move to Pasco or Kennewick. Judge Small's decision to cite him for contempt and send him to jail "was unfair," and he complained about being forced to work overtime at the post office to pay bills for attorneys and courts.

At that point, he finally said "maybe" he should talk to a lawyer. The interview was over.

The day before, at about 2 a.m. March 6 after the stabbing and the shootings, seven officers had gone to Bill Smith's residence, the mobile home up a driveway off Brisky Canyon Road. They surrounded it and a SWAT hostage negotiator called the Smith telephone number, in case Smith was holed up with his daughters. Colleen, 12 years old, answered and said her dad was not home. The four girls were taken by child welfare workers to a foster home in East Wenatchee. The house trailer was searched and some of the articles found included: Smith's notebook and diary on the kitchen table, the contents of which were not detailed; Smith's passport; four photos of Smith; a telephone list (no details); a black zip-up bag. Inside the bag were an empty Dan Wesson revolver box, some .357-caliber ammo, a toy cap gun, a leather pistol holster; a four-page letter (no details), some 20-gauge Federal shotgun shells, three boxes of Winchester .22 caliber cartridges, one box of .22-caliber Thunderbolt cartridges. Also found were a Springfield .22-caliber rifle; a Daisy air rifle; and a paperback, *On the Trail of the Assassins.* This non-fiction book, published in 1988 by Jim Garrison, was about an alleged conspiracy concerning the assassination of President John F. Kennedy.

Later on the morning of Friday, March 6, a detective and two child welfare workers talked to Bill Smith's daughters about the events of Thursday night, during the period before the violence began. They were not told of their mother's death or the search for their father. The girls said they went to the junior high basketball game with their dad and their uncle Bob. Colleen was on the team and normally her dad came to watch.

(One of Smith's neighbors told me he had seen Bill at the game, clipboard in hand, roaming the edge of the court and chiding Colleen if he thought she was not playing well.)

Later, at dinner on Thursday at home, the girls said their dad told them he might be called in that night to work and he would go because they needed the money. Erma, the woman from the Philippines, whom they called their "stepmother," telephoned and his daughters quoted Bill as telling her, "Things just aren't working out the way I planned." After the call, he sat quietly for a few minutes. He put them to bed.

They did think that during the last day or so, their dad had told them, "I love you," more often than usual. They also said that during the basketball game he bought them two soft drinks each instead of the usual one. He mentioned he had no money left to buy a newspaper, which was unusual. At this point in their narrative, the girls "were overcome with emotion" and left the room. Colleen came back with the handwritten note from her dad, which later was introduced at his trial. She had found it in her clothes, she said. Colleen did not understand what it meant, and had no idea where her dad was.

Chapter 5
Sanity & Verdict

The description of Bill Smith's capture was the end of the physical aspects of the trial–crime, chase and capture. What followed was more abstract, the testimony of a dueling psychologist and psychiatrist, expert witnesses hired to evaluate the mental state of the defendant and to argue whether his plea of insanity was valid. The main witnesses were forensic psychologist Dr. R.Bruce Duthie, besides Smith the only defense witness, and psychiatrist Dr. Verne Cressey, who testified for the prosecution. Duthie said Smith was legally insane. Cressey was forceful in his view that the defendant's main mental problem was a paranoid personality disorder, a condition that did not mean he was insane and thus free of criminal responsibility.

Dr. Duthie, a licensed psychologist, practiced in Richland, Washington. His doctorate was from Texas A&M, and he was a diplomate, American Board of Professional Psychologists and Forensic Psychologists. The state's witness, Dr. Cressey, a graduate of Northwestern University's school of medicine, became a psychiatrist after practicing medicine for six years in Tekoa, a small town in eastern Washington. After practicing in Spokane for 27 years, in 1986 he joined the forensic psychiatry staff at Eastern State Hospital, a state mental institution located in Medical Lake near Spokane.

In summary, Duthie's diagnosis was that Smith had a paranoid personality and a psychotic delusional disorder. Furthermore, when Smith committed the crimes he was unable to distinguish between right and wrong. These were mental disabilities that meant legal insanity. Duthie reached these conclusions after reading court documents and talking with Smith for about four hours at Eastern State Hospital where Smith was being held for a mental evaluation. In addition, Smith completed a written questionnaire called the Minnesota Multiphasic Personality Inventory, a standard approach for evaluating mental status.The results bolstered his diagnosis, Duthie said.

At first, the psychologist thought Smith might not have a full-blown mental disorder, perhaps he was "just" paranoid, which would not be a serious mental illness, or at least not a problem that would rise to the level of legal insanity. The psychologist's diagnosis of a delusional disorder, which is more serious, was based on his belief that Smith had "an ongoing and comprehensive delusion" about certain women. Smith referred to them as "women libber bitches," Duthie said.

"He felt that these people had, in using his (Smith's) words again, brainwashed his wife, or his ex-wife. And he felt these people were controlling the church his ex-wife went to and that they had influence in the court system. And that they were plotting to have his children removed from his custody and placed in the custody of his ex-wife."

Another factor was Smith's preoccupation and obsession with the abortion his wife had in 1988, which Smith expressed as "feeling like she had killed his child."

Duthie recited a long list of wrongs Smith believed had been perpetrated against him since his wife filed for divorce in 1988.

"He believed that people who evaluated the family were for the most part on his ex-wife's side and that they were also plotting against him to take his children away. He believed that his attorneys as well as opposing attorneys were all in a conspiracy with the magistrates and judges to cause his financial ruin for their own economic benefit.

"He believed that one of the counselors was having a sexual relationship with his ex-wife. He believed that this counselor was having secret counseling sessions with the children for the purpose of turning them against him. He believed that members of his own family, including his mother, were financially supporting the custody battle that his ex-wife and he were involved in.

"He believed that there was a general conspiracy by magistrates and judges against fathers coming into court in custody matters."

Dr. Duthie said he had gleaned this information from court records and that these records were consistent with what Smith had told him during the four-hour interview at Eastern State Hospital and, in addition, was similar to Smith's trial testimony. Furthermore, Smith did not know the difference between right and wrong when he killed his ex-wife, Duthie said.

Smith did not believe the law "was a rightful authority over him and believed that he was truly right morally and in other ways when he killed his ex-wife," Duthie testified. The delusion was connected "specifically" to the Chelan County court system.

Regarding his diagnosis of paranoid personality disorder, Dr. Duthie said Smith showed several classic symptoms. These included: an expectation without "sufficient basis" that he would be exploited or harmed by others; hidden or threatening meanings are read into "benign remarks or events"; grudges are kept and fancied insults or slights are not forgiven; a reluctance to confide in others because "of unwarranted fear" that the confidence will be used against him; and quickness to react with anger.

Prosecutor Riesen, in his cross-examination, predictably expressed deep skepticism of Duthie's evaluation and diagnosis. The cross-examination was tense from the beginning. Riesen asked Duthie why he had not included his mental status evaluation of Smith in his written report filed with the court. "Isn't that an accepted practice for a psychologist doing a forensic examination to do a mental status examination of the defendant?"

"It may or may not be. I mean, it's kind of up to the person doing it," Duthie said.

"Why didn't you put it in the report?"

"Because I didn't. Because I didn't," Duthie replied.

Riesen said he considered it significant to know what Smith's mental status was, especially if the defendant had pleaded insanity. Riesen asked about Smith's behavior during Duthie's interview. The psychologist said he was lucid, was not having auditory hallucinations and was not acting in a bizarre fashion. Riesen asked when Duthie had decided Smith was incapable of telling right from wrong.

"I don't remember. I don't remember," Duthie said.

Riesen wondered about Duthie's diagnosis that Smith was delusional, with a main factor being that Smith "was preoccupied and obsessed" that his wife had an abortion. Duthie said Smith's obsessive preoccupation with the abortion was not normal. Riesen was surprised that Duthie thought obsessive thoughts about abortion were unusual.

The prosecutor also wondered why Duthie had used Smith's reported use of the term "women libber bitches" as a reason to describe Smith as delusional. "Well, isn't it true, sir, a lot of folks in society probably could be termed male chauvinist and would use the term 'women libber bitches'?"

"I normally don't hear those words, at least in the part of society that I frequent," Duthie replied, but did agree the term might be based on reality.

Riesen didn't think something could be called a delusion if it were possibly based on reality. Duthie responded by diving into a textbook definition of delusion, meaning a delusion that "fits into a belief system," something called "a meta-belief system."

Riesen moved on, asking the psychologist about Smith's supposed delusion about his ex-wife. Duthie said Smith may not have had a delusion that was specific to his ex-wife, but rather she was part of a false belief system. Ann Smith Patrick, Duthie said, was seen by her ex-husband "as a pawn at the mercy of a corrupt system."

Duthie did not consider that Smith's supposed paranoid personality disorder was a condition that would relieve Smith of criminal responsibility. "Of course, there could be cases where it could, but I don't think it applies here."

Next was the matter of whether Smith could tell right from wrong. Riesen suggested that the fact that Smith fled after stabbing his ex-wife indicated he knew he had done something wrong, "that society would condemn the act that he undertook." Duthie agreed Smith understood killing his ex-wife was a crime.

But, Duthie added: Smith was not able to tell right from wrong because his experiences and delusions about the judicial system led him to believe that the judicial system was not acting in a fair and impartial way and therefore had no authority over him. "Therefore, he did not recognize or doesn't recognize–and from what I can see, from what I saw of his testimony–still doesn't recognize or believe that he was wrong."

The next day, a Friday, before the jury members were present, and before the next expert witness took the stand, the prosecutor wanted to straighten out the matter of Bill Smith's forceful statement the day before that he was not crazy. Riesen didn't think Smith had formally withdrawn his insanity plea, but wanted more discussion, which continued out of the presence of the jury.

Defense attorney Dan Arnold said the insanity plea was not being withdrawn. He noted that a delusional disorder would make a person with the disorder feel they were not insane. "If they knew they were insane, they wouldn't have the disorder. It's sort of a Catch-22. It's a paradox."

Arnold had consulted his client and they decided the insanity plea would remain. "Bill's simple statement that he is not insane is just that, that's his opinion."

Judge Wardell wanted to hear that from the defendant. Smith said, "I don't want to withdraw anything. You know, we're at trial, so let's, you know, go on with the trial … . I don't want to withdraw anything."

After a brief recess, the jury was called in and testimony resumed.

The state's witness, Dr. Verne Cressey, was 71, a Marine fighter pilot in World War II, folksy and plain-spoken. He had been part of Bill Smith's mental evaluation team at Eastern State Hospital, where Smith had been under 24-hour observation for eight days.

Riesen asked Cressey for his evaluation.

"Well, mental status is basically what it says. And what our findings were, well, the way you describe a person is kind of interesting. I could describe–I hope I can, anyway–Mr. Smith's mental state yesterday and compare it with what we had before (at Eastern State)," Cressey said.

"Well, yesterday (referring to Bill Smith's two hours of testimony), Mr. Smith was seemingly healthy, fairly well developed, well nourished, but a rather somewhat sad adult male who appears to be about his stated age. Serious, rather rigid in his thinking. He had no problem in really expressing himself. His speech was normal. He spoke with a kind of regular rate and rhythm."

Cressey said Smith showed no delay in relating his thoughts, but answered questions reasonably logically and reasonably clearly.

"His demeanor was that of a reasonably well-educated man. He is a college graduate, and this was reflected in his speech. His voice was generally clear. You could understand what he had to say. He didn't hesitate particularly, but there were some characteristic motions. I noticed yesterday frequently he would shake his head from side to side as if he was somewhat bewildered and couldn't quite understand why all this had happened to him. He made, well, he appeared to be a rather humorless man. I didn't see any humor yesterday. He appeared a little depressed. His ability to communicate was really, really fairly good.

"Now, in his thought content he seemed to be really focused on the legal system, on his children, showing a lot of care and concern about the children. Not showing much care or concern about himself. Not showing much care or concern about his ex-wife, what had happened to her. Showing to me little or no remorse about the whole thing."

Dr. Cressey, referring to Smith's thought processes, said the defendant "appeared to me to be a perfectly intact individual. He did not appear at all to be psychotic or crazy or off the wall or anything like that."

Smith was logical in his answers and did not "wander off in tangents," he said.

Cressey spoke of delusions, giving a quickie primer on that mental disorder. "Now, delusions are kind of a false belief. They're not based on reality, and they're not a superstitious belief."

A person might feel that four leaf clovers might bring good luck, although usually it doesn't work that way. "We all share that. That is not a delusion; that is a superstition that we all share."

"But, a delusion is a false belief not based on reality. Like if I think that the judge is bugging me and trying to put thoughts in my head, that's a delusion–because she is not bugging me and she's not putting thoughts in my head. But, that's a delusion."

"We found no real delusions in this man. What we did find were kind of some pervasive attitudes, rather unwarranted tendencies on his part to blame everybody else for his difficulties, to feel they were picking on him, that he was an innocent victim of circumstances. We saw a lot of that thought content running through his mind, but it didn't reach the point of what we generally refer to as delusional thinking."

Cressey said Smith was not hallucinating and was not hearing voices.

"Now, as far as his feeling state is concerned, he looks sad. He looks depressed. But, it doesn't reach the point of a real serious depression. This man has had a big disaster in his life. He lost his kids, lost his liberties. His wife is no longer here. He no longer can see his kids, so he's been through a disaster, and he is logically depressed."

Cressey said Smith's orientation was good. "He knew the basics, such as what day it is and where he is and that he was charged and on trial. His memory was good. He has major strengths as well, including a good education and ability to communicate. He has a brother he likes and he likes children," Cressey said, and added Smith worked right up to the time "that this happened."

Riesen stopped the mental health lecture and asked Cressey for his diagnosis.

Cressey said Smith was not a paranoid schizophrenic and was not suffering from a delusional disorder, both serious conditions. He did suffer from depression, an "adjustment disorder," which was not considered a major depression. The main diagnosis was "a paranoid personality, which is life long." The symptoms are fairly simple, defined as attitudes of "an isolated individual."

"You kind of expect that people are going to exploit you; people are going to get you. You tend to be kind of a lonely, isolated individual. You won't get close to people. You're afraid of the loyalty of your friends. You can't even trust them. You read all kinds of meanings into people's remarks, twist them around. You get insulted real easily, and you become very unforgiving about the insults and bear grudges. You become reluctant to confide in people because you can't trust them and it's going to come back and haunt you.

"You feel easily slighted and quick to become angry. Often you question the fidelity of your spouse, often accuse them of having affairs. This is the personality disorder; it's just a life-long description of what the person is like."

The disorder, Cressey said, does not necessarily cause the paranoid person any stress personally, but it is likely to cause stress to other people because they have to live with it.

The descriptions of a classic paranoid personality by both Dr. Duthie and Dr. Cressey matched descriptions of Bill Smith by people who knew him and resembled some of his behavior during the long court fight with his ex-wife. Paranoid personality disorder, Cressey said, is a widespread type of paranoia and extends to many aspects of the life of the person who has it.

Cressey ruled out schizophrenic paranoia for Smith. That's a major illness involving a profound break with reality. Symptoms, he said, might include a feeling the judge is putting thoughts in your head or the jury is pulling thoughts out of your head, or that "the clock and television might be sending you messages. That is a serious, serious illness. He does not have that at all."

Another serious mental illness that Smith did not have, Cressey said, is a delusional disorder. Such a person may have a perfectly normal appearance and a normal way of conversing, except they have an area of their life that is delusional. For instance, Cressey said, they might complain of bugs under their skin. They go to doctor after doctor for help and the doctor might rub ointment on their skin or give them fake X-ray treatments. Otherwise, they often are perfectly normal and pleasant, except for that one major delusion.

Riesen noted that Dr. Duthie the day before had said Bill Smith had a delusional disorder. "Would you agree with that?" the prosecutor asked.

"No, I don't agree," said Cressey, "because, first of all, Mr. Smith's delusions revolve around the legal system, around social and health services, around his wife, around the people in the church. And it's widespread, and it's not one but a whole bunch of delusions. I think they're really his unwarranted attitude toward people. And I don't think they're at all psychotic or at all crazy. I don't think so. I think that is within the realm of normal thinking."

"But if you want to call them delusions, his are not unlikely delusions, they're likely. This man has been in court for four years. And this man has been doing things like he said yesterday–one remark I wrote down was, 'I told the judge to shut up.' You tell the judge to shut up, you're going to be on that judge's list, you know, and you're going to be picked on a little bit."

Smith probably was picked on, Cressey said. His delusions likely were based on fact. "He's been in court so much, everybody is sick of him. He's a threatening man. He certainly was aggressive with his wife, had scared her to death."

Delusional disorder just didn't fit, Cressey said.

"In this case I don't see the man being at all psychotic. He's a very rigid man. He's controlling and all that, but he knows what he's doing." Smith would not have been able to hold jobs as long as he did if he were delusional since people with this problem are noted for bizarre remarks and odd behavior.

Riesen asked if Smith knew right from wrong when he killed his ex-wife and shot three people, a key question that pertained to at least part of the definition of legal insanity.

"Yes," Cressey replied, "I think he did."

Smith decided on several occasions not to shoot someone, Cressey said. He did not shoot Joe Halliday when Halliday came home from work and found Smith in his house. Cressey said Smith debated with himself whether to shoot Halliday and decided not to because Halliday had not done anything to him.

He went to the Cashmere residence of the Rev. Glenn Kennedy, Ann Smith Patrick's pastor, but decided not to shoot him because Kennedy's children were nice to his daughters. "So, I think this tells right from wrong, both legally and morally," Cressey said.

(I asked Smith in 2012 about Cressey's comments about Smith's decision not to shoot the Rev. Kennedy. After venting his dislike for Cressey, Smith said Kennedy was "a real backstabber," and went off on a tirade about Kennedy's supposed effort to recruit Smith's daughters for his church, which included very few young people. Smith did not directly answer my question, which was not unusual, but did imply he had spared Kennedy because his daughter "seemed to be trying to be a good young person.")

If Smith hadn't known he had done wrong that night, Cressey said he would have done what he did and then gone home. Smith had no plans to go home.

Smith's description of chanting "I must, I must, I must," while stabbing his ex-wife indicated something else, Cressey said. "That takes a little courage to do that if you know it's wrong. So he chanted and had a hard time with it but still did it." He also testified he did not like what he was doing and referred to having been a butcher, which meant he could use a knife silently "and it would be a quick kill." These comments mean Smith was aware that what he was doing was wrong, Cressey said.

(In one of his letters from prison Bill Smith told me his opinion of Dr. Cressey. I had asked him what he thought of the psychiatrist. Smith's reply: "As for Cressey, that little dried-up weasel; everything he said was a leading question and he was trying to drive that interview (at Eastern State Hospital) just where he wanted it to go, and he did want me to know how proud he was to be a big shot in his Methodist social so-called church and he let me know I was a dirty S.O.B." because of what Smith had done to the other Methodists, meaning the LaVignes. Smith wrote that Cressey's "taller, skinny partner (Dr.

Richard Dennie) knew what was going on and he was fair and professional." Dr. Cressey died in 2002, aged 81.)

Dr.Richard Dennie, a psychologist and a colleague of Cressey, was part of the team that evaluated Smith at Eastern State Hospital, with Dennie spending more time on the personality tests, which Smith completed. Dennie told the court he considered the personality tests invalid. Some of Smith's scores, he said, looked as if he were trying to seem sicker than he was.

After some squabbling between the lawyers over the test results, Judge Wardell gave her instructions to the jury. The trial was close to winding up, except for closing statements, jury deliberation and verdict.

In their closing statements, Riesen and Arnold agreed the night of March 5th and the early morning of the next day were a terrible time. As Arnold put it: "A night of terror. A night of horror." He didn't think Riesen would disagree and he didn't. But, they parted company on one major detail. Was Smith insane?

"It was also a night of insanity. There is no other way to understand what went on," Arnold said.

Riesen was blunt in his rejection. "It was murder fueled by hate, fueled by vengeance." Anyone, he said, who heard the coroner describe Ann Smith Patrick's knife wounds or heard the emergency room physicians testify in detail about the life-threatening injuries of Rebecca Hovda and Duane and Jane LaVigne would not mistake motivation for anything but hate and vengeance.

Riesen said there was no question about Smith's intent when he stabbed his ex-wife. "There was hate behind that knife." Smith continued stabbing until he had torn a hole in her throat, until "he had cut out the whole right side of her throat" and Mrs. Patrick bled to death. "She was dead in her bed."

The prosecutor was equally blunt in commenting on Smith's statements that he did not intend to kill Mrs. Hovda or the LaVignes when he shot them at close range with a 20-gauge shotgun. "Ladies and gentlemen, that is absolutely ridiculous." He said Smith had been in the military. He was familiar with firearms. He hunted.

It was "absolutely absurd" that he thought shoving the shotgun into Mrs. Hovda's abdomen and pulling the trigger would only injure her. The wound was "a grapefruit-sized hole," he said. He shot Duane LaVigne at a range of four to six feet, and then shot Mrs. LaVigne in the throat, missing her carotid artery by scant millimeters. "Are those the actions of someone who does not intend to kill somebody?"

Why did Smith use the shotgun against three of the victims? Another example of Smith's rational approach, said Riesen. He used the knife because it was silent and he did not think anyone would be home except the victim. But, more people were living at the Hovda and LaVigne residences. "It's a lot easier," Riesen said, "to control multiple people with a gun than it is with a knife. If you've got a knife and there's a man in the house, he might jump you. He might be bigger than you. He might take it away from you. But he's not going to take that shotgun away from you because anybody that sees a shotgun pointed at their face is going to back up.

"Try it in the jury room. Point that gun at each other, see what it makes you feel like. It makes you back up. Perfectly rational thinking choice."

Riesen said there was no question that Smith had committed the acts he was charged with, and he had admitted committing them. He was "cold and calculating."

These crimes were done with criminal intent and premeditation, Riesen told the jury, and the state had supported the four charges filed against Smith beyond a reasonable doubt.

In regard to Smith's plea of insanity, Riesen said, the defense must prove by a preponderance of the evidence that he is insane. The jury must decide that a mental disease or defect has affected the defendant's mind to such an extent that he was unable to perceive the nature and quality of the acts he is charged with, or was unable to tell right from wrong in connection with these specific acts.

"Ladies and gentlemen," Riesen said, "that is known as the M'Naghten Rule. This is a rule that evolved a long time ago under the law in England. One of the basic premises of the criminal law in the criminal law system is that a person must do two things in order to be guilty of a crime. They must have committed an act, a physical act–in this case murder or the attempted murders, actually–but they must be able to form a criminal intent. They must be able to know under this M'Naghten test that what they're doing is wrong and what kind of an act it is."

No one was arguing that Smith did not know what he was doing when he killed Mrs. Patrick or shot Mrs. Hovda and the LaVignes, Riesen said. That leaves the question of right and wrong. Insanity is not a medical definition and is not defined by expert witnesses. The decision is left to the jury using common sense and life experiences and consideration of the evidence heard in court.

Riesen asked the jury to take a look at the evidence heard in court. Smith planned the crime. "That's intent. That's legal right and wrong."

The prosecutor said Smith wrote notes to his girls, good-bye notes, because he knows he will be in trouble and may be killed. He packed provisions. He wanted to survive. He was rational. He tries to find out where Judge Bridges lives by going to a local post office. He doesn't like Judge Bridges, who has "messed with him one too many times."

Riesen talked about the weapons, the sawed-off shotgun, easier to carry under his coat. The knife was quieter, a better choice if only one person was in the house. Even in surrendering to the police, Smith was rational. If somebody had a gun pointed at you and told you not to move, a rational person would not move. Smith didn't move. He even asked for a lawyer. Smith himself denied he was crazy.

The treatment team at Eastern State Hospital observed Smith for eight days "and never saw one piece of psychotic behavior from him."

"His testimony was scary. You heard him talk about killing his wife ... He knew how to kill someone with a knife." Riesen said Smith was antisocial, no question about that. "This defendant is not crazy; he is dangerous, scary."

The only way Smith could accomplish what he wanted, which was to control the situation in an absolute way, was to eliminate those who stood in his path. The only way he could eliminate them "from the picture, his picture of life, was to kill them," Riesen said. He asked the jury to find Smith guilty on all four counts, thanked them and sat down.

Judge Wardell thanked him and suggested that the jurors take a stand-up break. Nobody else, just the jurors. She admonished people in the audience to stop talking and sit down. She asked the jurors to direct their attention to defense attorney Arnold's closing statement.

Arnold spent little time on close examination of the legal aspects of Smith's insanity defense. He bored in on what he believed was his client's motive, deluded as it may have been.

"This man actually believed that what he was doing was right. His children were in jeopardy, he thought. That is the delusion. He thought his children would be killed. One was killed already, by his understanding. He was afraid of what would happen. He thought–you understand no one is saying this is true–but it was true in his mind that his wife, who had already killed as he saw it one child, had told him she would kill."

In his testimony, Smith had told Riesen under cross-examination that he kept the shotgun away from his wife because she worried about hurting their children with it. "She didn't want me to show her how to load the guns ... because she was worried that when she shot herself she would shoot the kids first ... ."

"This was a night of insanity fueled by delusions," Arnold said. Smith thought everybody, including judges and lawyers, were out to harm him and his children, and only one way existed to protect them. It didn't matter whom he talked to, psychiatrists, psychologists, social workers, jurors, he always told everybody the same thing: he did what he had to do.

He thought he was gutless, Arnold said, a weakling, because he had not acted sooner. "Isn't that crazy? He thought what he did was right and he should have done it sooner."

Arnold said another aspect of Smith's testimony "is shattering to any notion of sanity" in Smith's case. The attorney told the jury the coroner's testimony about the injuries to Mrs. Patrick and the autopsy photos "was awful stuff." And Smith admitted it all. "He even told the psychologist and psychiatrists about going after other people. The judge. He had a deer rifle for the judge."

But, even after all that, Arnold said, his client insisted he was not dangerous. "He's the most dangerous man in the county. He's proved that."

"He's not dangerous. What he did was right. He accomplished what he needed to do. The girls are safe; it's over. The war is over. He was at war, and it's over. He's a prisoner of war. If this isn't crazy, if this isn't insanity, what is?"

Arnold told the jury that Smith "had absolutely no faith in the legal system; that to him it was corrupt. Now, I'm a lawyer. I'm part of the legal system. I'm Bill's lawyer. And I'm not going to tell you that the legal system is corrupt. It has a few problems, and there are some people in it that may be corrupt–it happens in any profession, in any organization, in any agency, in any institution. But every single judge was corrupt? Every lawyer on either side was corrupt? That is a delusion."

There is no argument that Smith intended to kill his ex-wife, Arnold said. "He didn't want to do it. He wouldn't do it. Finally–finally he summoned his courage to do what he saw as his duty, what he saw as the right thing." He did it to protect his children. It was his duty. He had no faith in the legal system."

"Now, there isn't anybody in this courtroom with the exception of one person who would tell you it was right, that it was his duty."

But, on the three charges of attempted murder, Arnold said there was no intent to kill; there was intent to injure. He shot each person once. Once, of course, was way too many, "one hundred times too many." But, Smith shot once with a weapon that he saw as a gun that would not kill them. He thought shortening the barrel would lower its power. Smith called that "a gross miscalculation. Boy, was it." Arnold said Smith aimed for the abdomen, not the head. He used No. 6 birdshot instead of something possibly more lethal, such as No. 4, which he had in his ammunition storage at his house. Arnold got into the physics of shotgun pellet "dispersal" and foot-pounds of force based on gauge, shot size, barrel length and distance to the target. This discussion concluded that barrel length and shot size probably weren't significant because the range between Smith and his victims was only a few feet.

It was intent that should matter to the jury, Arnold said, and Smith's intent was not to kill, it was to wound.

Compared to the prosecution's expert witnesses, Drs. Cressey and Dennie, defense witness Dr. Duthie, was a trained and qualified expert in forensic psychology, Arnold said. He described Dr. Cressey, as "a fine and pleasant man" who had been interested in forensic psychiatry for 20 years but never was board certified in the field. Furthermore, Dr. Dennie didn't have the full credentials of a forensic psychologist either, as Dr. Duthie did. They simply did not have the full expert background to evaluate Smith's performance on the multiple-personality tests administered at the mental hospital.

These prosecution experts did not have the knowledge and experience to call Smith crazy, Arnold said. Dr. Duthie, the defense witness, decided

Smith was suffering from a delusional paranoid disorder, a necessary diagnosis to support the insanity plea. The events that triggered Smith's delusions about the legal system likely began in 1988 or 1989, which made Smith think the system was corrupt and unjust and it was up to him to save his children.

Bill Smith "did what he had to do," Arnold said, and sat down.

In a brief reply, Riesen said he would not "dignify" the defense's argument that Smith did not want to kill anybody when he fired the shotgun. "This is patently ridiculous."

Riesen said, referring to Arnold's comments about Smith's delusions, that the test is legal insanity. Did he know right from wrong? The jury, he said, decides who is legally insane. "I don't think Mr. Smith was ever delusional."

A bit more legal back and forth, and the case went to the jury.

Jury deliberation began at about 5 p.m. Friday, stopped a little before 9 p.m. and resumed the next morning at 9 a.m. for another 90 minutes or so. The verdicts of guilty on all counts were read at 11 a.m. Smith's plea of insanity had been rejected.

Smith sat, arms folded, as the verdicts were read. The *World's* story said he had "a slight, wry smile" as he heard the verdict. He told his attorney he was sorry the jury had to hear the details and that he "didn't hold anything against them." Leaving the courtroom, he took a tissue out of his pocket and clenched it, but didn't use it.

Rebecca Hovda and Ann Patrick's widowed husband, Bob, were in court, as well as other family members and friends. They cried silently as Judge Wardell read the verdicts. "I think justice was served today," Bob Patrick told the *World's* reporter, Jeanette Marantos.

He had not attended the trial until the jury's verdict came in. At his wife's funeral in March, Patrick had said both he and Ann expected she would die the way she did, killed by her ex-husband, but she refused to leave Cashmere because that would mean leaving her daughters.

Ms. Hovda sat through the entire trial and cried a long time after the verdict. "I had a lot of closure to do. This helped."

After the jurors were dismissed, they declined to be interviewed. Judge Wardell told reporter Marantos: "It seems I see the bad side of people a lot and this was the bad of the bad. He's going to be in prison for a long time."

Sentencing was set for September 23.

Chapter 6
Sentence & Appeal

Bill Smith had been convicted and a date set for his sentencing. First, though, there was the pre-sentence investigation, known in the law and justice trade as "the PSI." This document, in Smith's case put together by Paul Bird, a Department of Correction's community corrections officer in Wenatchee, is sort of a briefing for the judge, and includes interviews with the convicted person and "impact" letters from victims as well as other concerned persons. It also may include information on sentencing guidelines and the investigator's recommendation on sentencing. The judge decides the severity of the sentence, based on the charge and sentencing guidelines.

A thorough PSI is something like a consensus of the community's opinion on what the fate of the convicted person should be. In Smith's case, the consensus was fairly predictable. Smith was viewed as remorseless, and a definite danger to society. The three victims were united in describing the awful effect Smith's crimes had on them personally and on their family. They would never feel safe if Smith were released, since he had "boasted" he would finish what he had started if given the chance. Rebecca Hovda said she was aware Smith's list of intended victims was a long one, "but I live with the knowledge I was at the top of the list."

Bird included letters from Bill Smith's brother Robert and another from Smith's father Bob and stepmother Delores. Bob's letter, quoted in detail earlier in this work, emphasized he loved his brother, but "hate what he has done." Smith's parents said Bill's strengths were his devotion to his daughters, his pride, and his belief in fairness and justice. Pride, though, also was a major weakness, and contributed to his reluctance to ask for help to cope with the stresses in his life. They believed his fear of losing his daughters led to the crimes. They reacted to the crimes with "horrid disbelief," and felt their family had been destroyed in the aftermath. It was too late to help Bill, but they hoped the court system would accept some responsibility and never again allow a similar case to go so far.

No one wrote a letter recommending mercy. The impact letters were severe. Descriptions of Smith were unforgiving, with "fiend" and "monster" being two examples. One writer, an older woman who assumed she was on Smith's "list," told Judge Wardell a lenient sentence resulting in release from prison "would be a great danger to me and the entire community of Cashmere."

Another woman knew Smith in a casual way before his rampage. Her letter to the judge described Smith, when she first met him, as being "reticent and shy, a concerned father, a perfect gentleman." She said if she had not been aware of his behavior in the divorce/custody fight, "I might have been fooled … Bill Smith is clever and crafty and intelligent."

"Ann's friends, and I count myself among them, will always be at risk if he is ever released," she wrote.

Another woman, who did not describe her connection with Smith, said he was "an intelligent, clever, devious, tenacious man," whose "unrelenting nature makes it obvious" that if he were ever free the lives of anyone connected to his children or late wife "will be in jeopardy."

Not exactly expressions in support of leniency.

Investigator Bird's PSI interview with Smith was a rehash of trial testimony, except for an odd digression by the guilty man. He related his version of the Salem witch trials in the Massachusetts Bay Colony during the 1690s, during which 20 persons were executed, 19 of them for being witches, a historical incident viewed as an example of extreme and widespread hysteria. Smith compared Judge Bridges to the "activists" who led the campaign to root out and execute the alleged witches. Smith implied that "experts" and "greedy lawyers" were part of the conspiracy to destroy people who stood up to the corrupt court system. He blamed a prominent Puritan pastor, Cotton Mather, for much of the injustice. It was clear who and what Smith was talking about in his parable.

In his PSI statement to Bird, Smith included what stands as a heartfelt–although cruel—summary of his view of the crimes:

"I was blessed with five wonderful and precious little daughters, and I was forced to stand by and allow my youngest to be murdered in a terrible and disgusting manner. I swore to God that I would protect my four surviving little girls. On March 5, 1992, I went to war, and my ex-wife was stabbed to death, and three of her "cult followers" were wounded. My girls are saved and protected. They get to have a good education, be active in church and participate in good positive activities; and finally I feel so good about myself."

Another Smith comment that summed up his attitude more succinctly was when he told Bird he had wanted "to be left the fuck alone" to raise his children in the best way he knew how.

Bird concluded his Smith interview portion by saying that Smith "cooperated fully with me."

The sentencing recommendation from Bird was that Smith be given an exceptional sentence, which amounted to 126 years. Aggravating circumstances, required under state law for an exceptional sentence, included: victims were incapable of resistance; a firearm was involved in three of the four crimes; deliberate cruelty occurred; Smith's threat to finish what he started if released; his total lack of remorse.

The sentencing hearing before Judge Wardell took place Sept. 23, as scheduled. This hearing would be Smith's final public appearance and afforded him another chance to state his case for murder, and to display his characteristically defiant sarcasm. Otherwise, the hearing featured a request for an exceptional sentence from Prosecutor Gary Riesen, a plea for a lower sentence from defense attorney Dan Arnold (accompanied by an impromptu movie review), and a sternly worded decision from Judge Wardell.

Riesen asked the judge to impose a 126-year sentence, the same consecutive sentence that was recommended by investigator Paul Bird. This "exceptional" sentence was compared to a "standard" combined sentence of from 65 to almost 87 years. The prosecutor's aggravating factors were similar to the ones cited in the PSI, and included "invasion of zone of privacy," meaning the victims' bedrooms. In non-legal language, Riesen described Smith's acts "as violent and probably as cold and calculating as anyone could imagine."

Smith should be responsible for restitution totaling $89,003.85, which was mostly medical expense for the victims and counseling costs, Riesen said.

Arnold began his argument for a lower sentence with a personal note. He thanked the surviving victims and their families, who "were very gracious to me, very courteous to me, which I appreciate, considering my role and how someone might view me in the case." He expressed his "deepest sympathy for the pain and the suffering and the loss" they suffered.

Arnold's surprise movie review was of *Mutiny on the Bounty*, the 1962 version with Marlon Brando, Trevor Howard and Richard Harris. Arnold had watched it the night before, the second time in about 30 years. One scene reminded him vividly of the upcoming Smith sentencing hearing. Captain Bligh, after the "incredible" 3,600-mile journey in an open boat following his crew's mutiny, was on trial in England. Bligh was acquitted, and the judge told him, "The articles of the admiralty cannot cover all contingencies." Hence, exceptions may be justified.

But, Arnold said, the next line really got his attention: "Justice must be written on the hearts of her captains." In this vein, Arnold wondered why an exceptional sentence should be handed down in Bill Smith's case. He said a range using a standard sentence of from 65 to 87 years would mean Smith would be between 104 and 126 years old when released. Even with the possibility of early release, he would be 94 to 113. Under the state's request of 126 years, Smith would be 165 years old.

Arnold said when he heard the state ask for an exceptional sentence, he heard "the voice of the mob." Even with a standard range, he said, the age of Smith's children would be in the 60s and "most of us will be dead." He admitted his reaction was emotional. "It's tempting in a case like this, of this kind of notoriety, to exceed the range to make some kind of statement, but it's not the law."

He repeated that "justice must be written upon the hearts of her captains" and sat down.

Judge Wardell told Smith he had the right to address the court before he was sentenced.

"Well, your honor, I, you know, kind of am astounded at this point of anything–you're going to tell me I have the right to do anything. I mean, after years and years and years, you know, of being denied the right of anything."

After that, in what by then was a familiar presentation, he delivered a rambling, but apparently sincere, series of accusations that divorced husbands had no rights and that children were similarly ignored by society. Even young prisoners he met in jail were "angry that their childhood had been stolen from them." He repeated his complaints against the Chelan County court and justice system, about how he tried to get help to protect his children, "and you guys spit in my face."

"Why wouldn't I go to war … when there is no law … I would have done anything at the time to get my kids out of the mess."

He said he finally had seen his daughters the day before the sentencing hearing. They were beautiful and healthy, well dressed, and living with "a very nice family, with a wealthy family."

"I can say, 'Yeah, you know, I didn't like a lot of the things that I did … but I'm not going to apologize in any way to anybody."

The bottom line, he told the judge, was that his "kids are taken care of," and that is all he "gives a damn about." He would be happy to ramble on, he said, but "You've obviously prepared a speech. You want to say your things to humble me and make me feel small and send me to prison. Well, that's fine, but that doesn't have much of an impact on me. My kids are safe, and my kids are going to be taken care of, that is the bottom line."

Judge Wardell did have a speech. She first denied she wanted "to belittle" the man in front of her, adding anything she said would be a waste of time. She denied Smith's accusation that the system didn't care about children. The judge accused Smith of harming his own children by his acts.

Then, she told him exactly what she thought of him and his crimes.

"After listening to you testify at trial, after reading everything that I have read in this file, after fully considering everything that I know that has gone on, there is one word, and it's frightening. You're frightening. You're also evil and manipulative."

Her words were a preview of what the sentence would be. She agreed with the prosecutor that a low sentence would not be appropriate. She also told the defense attorney he was wrong about her being influenced by "the mob mentality." Her concern was the number of aggravating factors that supported an exceptional sentence, which included the fact all victims were attacked in their homes, more specifically in their bedrooms, and she explained that courts have recognized a person's home is a place where they have a right to feel secure.

"Mr. Smith has absolutely no remorse for what he's done. He went out on a hunting trip, and his only remorse was that he didn't finish the job, didn't kill other people. To me, that is an egregious lack of remorse, and it stands out in my mind."

Another factor was deliberate cruelty. Ann Patrick bled to death, she said, and the struggle was furious. And, even though the judge said she didn't like the term, "Rebecca Hovda was gut shot, point-blank with a shotgun in her stomach." Hovda's children were in the house, another factor. In addition, the crimes were all premeditated, "with planning and sophistication."

"Quite frankly, I never want to see Mr. Smith out of prison," no matter how old he is, she said.

Judge Wardell proceeded to specify the sentences, to be served consecutively. She imposed 40 years for Ann Patrick's murder, 30 years in the Rebecca Hovda case, and for the LaVignes, each 27.5 years, a total of 125 years. The judge noted that although she had no say in the matter of where Smith was locked up, she wanted the Department of Corrections to know "this court suggests a maximum security facility."

The judge told Smith he had a right to appeal and asked him if he understood.

Smith's last comment in court: "Well, I don't know about my–if I have any rights, but I certainly–I would like to have a right to appeal for a fair trial with a real judge."

The Court: "Thank you, Mr. Smith."

Attorney Arnold and Bill Smith did file appeals in 1993 and 1994, with the state Court of Appeals, Division III, in Spokane. Smith's personally-written appeal was *pro se*, meaning he filed on his own behalf, without his attorney's assistance.

Arnold's formal legal brief was based on various arguments, including that the judge refused to dismiss jurors for cause, was biased and had a conflict of interest. Judge Wardell, he said, commented on evidence during the trial and imposed an improperly long sentence. The judge should not have penalized Smith for not showing remorse, Arnold said. His client had continued to claim innocence, which was his constitutional right.

Judge Wardell's comment during the sentencing hearing that Smith "was evil and manipulative was a moralizing remark," Arnold said. He said Judge Wardell's feelings were the real reason for the extreme sentence.

"She abused her discretion," he said.

The appeals judges agreed that an unusually large number of potential jurors lived in the two small towns near where the crimes had occurred and that very few of the prospective jurors were unaware of the case.

During selection of the jury, according to Chelan County court clerk minutes, 17 prospective jurors, from the original jury pool of 60, were acquainted with Duane LaVigne; 15 knew Jane LaVigne; seven knew Rebecca Hovda; two knew Ann Smith Patrick; seven were acquainted with Bill Smith. Twenty-nine had formed an opinion concerning guilt.

Even so, the three appeals judges said Judge Wardell was correct in denying a motion for change of venue and the record shows an impartial jury was selected. Her reasons for imposing exceptional sentences were justified. Smith's conviction was affirmed. No reversible error was noted.

Bill Smith's 41-page *pro se* supplemental brief, in general, followed his attorney's arguments, but included the comment that he had "no illusion" that the appeal would succeed. His arguments at times had a paradoxical tone. For instance, he said he was entirely innocent of the charges, but did not dispute he had murdered his ex-wife and shot three of her friends. Again, he said he felt good about himself "as a person," even though he disliked "many of the events I was forced to do."

Smith added a few of his own quirky notions, which showed his unwavering belief in the rightness of his actions. He did not contest the findings that he committed the acts he was charged with, but did express again his sense that he had done something good for his daughters. It was understandable that these factors did not impress the appeals judges as reasons to overturn his conviction and sentence.

Smith disputed the testimony of state psychiatrist Dr. Verne Cressey. The psychiatrist said Smith was not insane, partly because Smith knew right from wrong. Cressey noted, for instance, that Smith had been careful to commit his alleged crimes in the middle of the night and did his best to be as silent as possible. Smith said he was not worried about being quiet when he kicked in his ex-wife's back door and later shot three people.

"I had put four little children to bed and my main concerns were primarily with them, that they were taken care of and that they would be safely sleeping during whatever was going to happen that night and they would wake up to a bright new world, finished with the prolonged agony and suffering of a corrupt divorce court."

The firmness of his belief that he had done the right thing was in the phrase, almost poetic if it had been expressed in other circumstances: "they would wake up to a bright new world … ."

He continued to insist he had not intended to murder Ms. Hovda or the LaVignes. "I clearly had no intention to kill those people, that's why I only shot them with a light gun in a non-fatal area of their body." This argument, of course, conflicted with the testimony of the Wenatchee hospital's emergency room physicians as well as common sense.

Smith, as usual, was vivid and used harsh language: "The selection of my jury was unfair and stunk to high heaven and completely proved how corrupt Chelan County court really is." Smith denied he had ever said his only regret was that he had not finished the job. That alleged comment "was an untrue smear job," which may have resulted when "a fat, hostile woman nurse tried to put words in my mouth at Medical Lake." He told the nurse he didn't care if any of the people involved lived or died "as it was nothing to me."

Smith repeated his earlier comment "that everything is over; so many things have ended up way better that I could have possibly ever dreamed that they would."

One portion of his appeal was striking. He disputed the testimony of Dr. Gerald Rappe, the county coroner. Smith, who never denied he had killed Ann Smith Patrick, said Rappe's version of her death "was wild speculations" and "a grisly story" that was designed to "create ugly images in the jury's minds."

Smith said there was "no furious battle" as described by the coroner. The victim, he said, was not sleeping in the darkened room on her stomach, but on her side, apparently away from him. "I tried to make a number of quick, clean cuts to her neck. I panicked when her legs began to thrash some as I felt she might be in pain and I stabbed her twice through the back where I thought her heart was so that she would not feel any pain and not suffer ... I did every thing I could to make her death as quick and as painless as I possibly could. I was not there to hurt her, but on business I had to complete. My ex-wife never even woke up."

He denied the judge's finding of deliberate cruelty.

Rappe, said Smith, made up a false story about "wounds and fighting and violent activity, which just did not happen." Smith said Rappe was correct when he said death occurred quickly, "near death within a minute." Smith said he timed himself by the clock in his pickup. "I ran through her locked door and completed my business and ran back to my pickup in just six minutes."

It would be difficult to understand how members of a jury or the appeals judges would consider Smith's version of the homicide to be less "grisly" than what the coroner had described. Smith admitted the events "were ugly and heart-wrenching enough" without the coroner's "emotional and sensational mirage."

Smith argued that any suggestion he had planned the crimes well in advance because he had packed food in his hunting bag was "ridiculous." He said he had "a few old Aplet and Cotlet reject candy snack treats from the local Cashmere candy factory and some old crackers, which had been in my hunting bag for months." Furthermore, all he had for a coat on a chilly winter's night was a thin raincoat. He fully expected to be killed by the law officers in pursuit, so he saw no reason for an elaborate "escape attempt."

In his *pro se*, Smith seemed to travel far afield when he suggested Rebecca Hovda had "recruited and drawn" his ex-wife into a lesbian lifestyle before the 1988 divorce, a lifestyle that Smith said continued after the divorce. In addition, he said Judge Wardell "knew these issues would be raised and it is well known in the local community" that the judge herself "was closely linked" to lesbian activities through sporting organizations. It was not clear why these accusations surfaced, although Smith did say Judge Wardell wanted to conceal such issues from the jury.

As an example of what he viewed as the judge's "intimidation," which forced him to give "false answers to questions," Smith cited his reply during the trial when the prosecutor asked what he would have done if Ann Smith Patrick's new husband had been home on the night he killed his ex-wife. Smith's answer had been: "I probably would have shot him."

"The truth of the matter was that I entirely knew that women, such as my ex-wife, engaged in lesbian love affairs and did not sleep at night with their 'for show' husbands, and that the recent show marriage was a farce to try to make her look somewhat respectable in court proceedings for the on-going custody battles." Smith said Ann Smith Patrick's new husband lived in the Tri-Cities (Bob Patrick's job was in Pasco, about 130 miles from Wenatchee), "just as Hovda's husband would not live with her, but he lived all the way over in Minnesota."

(Jumping ahead, both Rebecca Hovda and Carol Wardell, interviewed later, laughed when asked about Smith's speculative remarks. Their detailed reactions will appear later in this story. Siri Woods, Chelan County court clerk, when asked about Smith's *pro se* "lesbian lifestyle" comments, said she did vaguely recall a few lesbian-related accusations during court civil hearings, but did not recall any interest on the part of the judges and the comments were not pursued by either side.

"But, Bill would do anything to put Ann's friends in a bad light," Woods said. "And, being the sort of man he is, he may have jumped to conclusions." Any affection shown between women may have made him think something sexual was going on, she said.)

Back to the *pro se*. Smith also added comments about his lawyer's performance.

"Mr. Arnold was a new lawyer to our area after just being awarded the public defender's contract and he did indeed try to do his best effort for my defense." Too many agencies, though, "put roadblocks in his way or suppressed evidence from him and hindered his efforts on my behalf in any way they could."

Smith did not elaborate.

When he offered advice, Smith said Arnold did not follow it. One example was asking his attorney to question Rebecca Hovda "about her involvement in my unborn baby's needless death."

Smith ended the critique of his lawyer with characteristic sarcasm. "I certainly liked him as a person; it was just too bad that Mr. Arnold went to school and became a lawyer."

Smith ended his appeal with a suggestion: "My children and myself should be registered with Amnesty International as political prisoners to a corrupt court system."

In their decision, the appeals judges said many of Smith's *pro se* arguments refer to evidence outside the record and "such evidence cannot be considered by this court." Smith's arguments added "little to the argument by counsel," and the trial court's findings "are adequately supported by the record." The appeals court judges could not find any evidence Judge Wardell had abused her discretion or had shown any bias against the defendant.

After the appeals court turned him down, Smith on his own behalf filed petitions for review. These were unsuccessful. Attorney Arnold left the case in late 1994 after Chelan County's payments for his services ended.

Bill Smith began his 125-year sentence at the state penitentiary in Walla Walla in late 1992, later was transferred to Airway Heights Corrections Center near Spokane and, at this writing, was at Coyote Ridge Corrections Center north of the Tri-Cities. Judge Wardell's recommendation for maximum security confinement was followed in the beginning at the state penitentiary, but later Smith was placed in medium-security custody. He apparently has been perhaps not a model inmate, but one who has not caused serious or repeated trouble for the prison system. Any chance he would enjoy a mitigation of his sentence or any form of early release seemed slim. The trial judge had emphasized he should be locked up forever, a request taken even more seriously when the man involved was not only a convicted murderer, but an admitted and remorseless hunter of judges and lawyers.

Chapter 7
Later

By 2000, when I began work on the Bill Smith story, it had been eight years since the crimes and trial, and even longer since the divorce and seemingly endless court fights. I lost momentum and put the project away in mid-2002 and two years later left Cashmere and moved back to Bellingham. But, I experienced a major revival of inspiration in late 2009 after a chance viewing of a TV interview about, of all things, the ancient Greek tragedy *Medea* by Euripedes. Almost a cosmic intervention, I thought. I had put the Bill Smith story aside, gone on to other things, never quite forgetting it, but never quite having the energy to continue. After *Medea,* I jumped back in, assembling and adding to what I had learned from the distant round of interviews and research.

By 2010, much time had passed since March 1992, plenty of time for sober reflection or forgetting. Some lives were seemingly on course, others had vanished into the quiet of cemeteries and one had almost disappeared in the near anonymity of prison routine.

Back in 2000 I had begun a round of interviews of the main characters, at least those willing to talk. Many rebuffed me, wanting to forget and move on, which was to be expected. Some had to be reminded of details. For others their recollections of events were as fresh as the day they happened.

I moved into the spacious second floor Cashmere apartment in September 2000. It was a comfortable place with big windows and a good view of the hills across the river, a carport for my '98 Honda and a shed for my 12-speed Raleigh. I rode the bicycle almost daily, in reasonable weather, into the canyons around Cashmere, excellent times for thinking about Smith and how to proceed. My main ride took me up Brender Canyon Road to the intersection with Brisky Canyon, near where Smith had lived with his family before March 1992. After I moved in, though, one of my first stops was a visit to Ann Smith Patrick's grave in the town cemetery across the road. This visit was the first of many, in the hope a ghostly Ann might whisper from wherever she had gone, and tell me the real story, at least her side. When a person is murdered, his or her version tends to be told by others, unless the victim conveniently has left a confessional journal behind.

Ann's grave is toward the cemetery's north end, four rows in from the narrow graveyard road. A flat, simple stone and economical message: "Loving wife and mother, Ann Patrick, July 10, 1955–March 6, 1992." My first thought was, "Loving wife?" Later, I realized "loving wife" referred to her marriage to Bob Patrick, not to Bill Smith. Ann never talked to me, in a ghostly whisper or any other way. The conversation was one-sided, with impossible questions from me. One was: "Why didn't you give up the court fight if you sensed your life could be in danger?"

This question probably was inspired by something court chief clerk Siri Woods had said in one of our real life conversations. "If you are playing Russian roulette, don't pull the trigger."

On the day after Memorial Day in 2001, I visited the grave again to check on how devoted Ann's friends had been on the day Americans remember the dead. At her grave, I saw two nice bouquets next to her stone and one long-stemmed rose on the stone itself. I brushed off the grass cuttings and went on my way.

One of the less gloomy places I frequented during my Cashmere life was Barney's Tavern and Café, a squat cinder block building with a deck for summer drinking and dining. Barney's was at one end of a block-long parking lot across from the post office. It was a Cashmere tradition, the best place in town for breakfast, and I took advantage of this feature by having a cheap breakfast there most mornings–almost always the same order. One hotcake and coffee for $2.15. Being a regular, I got to know Ginger Graves, the robust and outspoken woman who ran the place with help from her husband Gary, whose main job was operating heavy equipment. Ginger, in her mid-50s in 2000, became a good source for Cashmere lore, including the Bill Smith case.

Barney's was dimly lighted, bar and kitchen along one side and across the cavernous room big picture window views of the Cascades to the west.

My favorite spot was the far back table next to the window with an expansive look at pickups in the parking lot and mountains beyond. Mount Cashmere was one of the prominent peaks, elevation 8,501 feet. Big TV sets anchored each end of the room. Barney's was popular with early-rising pear and apple growers, called "ranchers," many of them in the geezer category, wearing caps with agricultural firm logos. They came in their big pickups, with the early birds lining up at the door for the pre-dawn opening. Very pre-dawn, between 3:30 and 4 a.m. six days a week. Sunday was banker's hours, with an 8 a.m. opening. A non-rancher regular was Duane LaVigne, one of Bill Smith's midnight victims. Customers poured their own coffee and made their own change. Coffee was 50 cents, a bottomless cup, and don't bother to ask for decaf, known contemptuously as "unleaded." One story about Barney's style was told by a young woman from California. One night, at the bar, she asked for Perrier. After Perrier was explained to the bartender, he said, "Lady, the only water we have here comes right out of the Wenatchee River."

Barney's conversation usually was about weather, politics, taxes, fruit prices, labor troubles, sports (high school, college, pro), illness, hospitalizations, deaths. One rancher usually brought his Hispanic foreman, but Hispanic and women customers were rare sights, except on Saturdays when women sometimes came in groups.

"Mexican" was the generic term for all orchard workers, no matter where they came from south of the border.

Sample comment: "That little Mexican who works for Valentine, boy, he can put on a picking demonstration. I've seen him in Goldens, and man, can he pick."

Walls were covered with fruit packing box labels–Icicle, Blue Star, Blewett Pass, Blue Bird, Empire Builder, Sapphire, Glacier Peak, Stemilt, Trout. Pears, apples, cherries. Signs posted by Ginger said: "Roosters crow, hens deliver the goods." "If mama is happy, everybody is happy." "Shoes required. Bras and panties optional." That's the sort of place it was.

Ginger, in the kitchen, yelled at a customer who had complained about slow service. "If you would order off the menu you would get your breakfast quicker. When I get the time I'm coming out there and kick your ass."

Occasionally, Ginger would come out and sit with me. I had been going to Barney's long before I lived in Cashmere because as a newspaper reporter in Seattle I would get assignments "east of the mountains." I would make it a point to stop in Cashmere for an expense account breakfast, something grander than a $2.15 hotcake and java. Ginger called the western half of the state across the mountains, "the wet side, the dark side" and the people who lived there were "206ers," the area code for Seattle.

She was only slightly acquainted with Bill Smith, who was not a Barneys' customer, but had seen him at sporting events. He had wanted one of her daughters to baby sit, but the girl never did. Ginger considered Smith "a brick or two short of a full load," but also wondered how a seemingly fairly normal man could become a murderer. Ginger did know the couple who had adopted the Smith girls and had become acquainted with the girls. She was fairly tight-lipped about details of their lives after 1992, except that they had regular chores and raised animals for 4-H. She said they had been raised right by their adoptive parents.

"They are all smart girls, well mannered. They learned responsibility." She added that the parents were "very protective" of them.

The morning after the homicide and shootings, the emergency medical aid crews came in for breakfast. She never understood how they could relate their experiences in so much awful detail and eat breakfast at the same time.

(Barney's closed in August 2011. There were tax troubles with the state and other factors. The following year the business was listed for sale. Ginger was 66 and taking it easy. Husband Gary was going strong, working as a heavy equipment operator in the North Dakota oil fields. The old-timers, Duane LaVigne among them, were having a hard time finding an early morning replacement for Barney's coffee and conversation.)

An important piece of the story challenged me–the four Smith girls. I did not know how to proceed with them. By the time I came on the scene all had the same last name, but it wasn't Smith. After 1992, they stayed in the Cashmere area, living up Nahahum Canyon in a ranch environment. All were adopted by a married couple, Jerry and Bea James, people who had known their dad for years, and had worked with him in the custom meat business. The girls did well in school, and by 2000 and beyond were in college, thinking of college or out of college and headed for adult life. I only met one, the youngest, and that was by accident. These girls posed a dilemma for me, an ex-newspaper reporter trained to get all sides of a story, no matter how difficult or hurtful or embarrassing. Much of my problem was expressed in Janet Malcolm's famous, at least among journalists, first two sentences in her fascinating little book, *The Journalist and the Murderer:*

"Every journalist who is not too stupid or too full of himself to notice what is going on knows that what he does is morally indefensible. He is a kind of confidence man, preying on people's vanity, ignorance or loneliness, gaining their trust and betraying them without remorse."

In general, I agreed with Malcolm, and wanted to avoid the worst of her description of the typical journalist's way of doing the job.

Early on, in my first conversations with Bill Smith, and in letters back and forth, he made it very clear his daughters were to remain outside the frame in any depiction of his case. He did not want them involved. He wanted them to be strictly left alone. I agreed, realizing quickly that if he ever learned I was badgering his daughters, he would cut me off. Without Smith, I knew there was not much of a story, certainly nothing beyond a true crime recitation of events and tiresome rehash of cop and similar interviews. I was not immune, though, to considering Malcolm's accusations of journalistic mendacity, meaning I could always consider moving on the daughters after I had drained Smith of what I needed. After all, what could he do about it?

I did try several times, in polite non-threatening letters, to get in touch with the adoptive parents. The idea was to get permission from the parents to meet with their daughters. These letters were not answered.

Another question was: Was there a story without a deeply-detailed account of the lives of the daughters? After all, in his view, Smith's crimes were motivated by selfless concern for his daughters' future. Was I obligated to corner them, eventually, and somehow convince them to tell me their side, their reactions and emotional responses?

I finally decided to pretty much leave them alone. I decided to rise above the mendacity described by Janet Malcolm as an integral part of most journalism, the part about gaining trust, followed by betrayal. This decision to avoid Malcolm's trust-betrayal combination pertained as well to Bill Smith. I had agreed to avoid badgering his girls and would stick to my pledge.

These decisions had some basis aside from nobility. What difference did it make how the daughters turned out? If they had done well, did that mean Smith could read the future and was right to murder their mother? If they turned out poorly, did that mean Smith was totally off the beam, was totally wrong, and deserved everything he got? I decided the emotional impact of the crimes should be left to the girls to express. I figured that was their story. Let them tell it.

I did check around a bit after 2010 and learned that all the girls, by now young women, ranging in age from the late twenties to early thirties, apparently were living their lives in a reasonable fashion. None seemed to be troubled in any way remarkably different from the general run of us humans.

The only journalism I ever saw that mentioned the girls, except the stories of the crimes and the trial, was an article about their mother's funeral in *The Wenatchee World.* They sat together in the front pew of the church, flanked by state social workers responsible for their care. The four blonde girls got up at one point and walked together to the front of the church. All of them were crying, and all but the youngest, six years old, said a few words about their mother, mostly to the effect of how much they would miss her.

I learned that by the time I took up the Smith project again in 2010, a couple of the girls were married, were to be married or had been married. One was a school teacher in Arizona, another worked for an accounting firm in Yakima, Washington. One was described as "a free spirit," who may have vanished for the time being into Mexico. She is the same one who may have visited her dad in prison, a visit that apparently was not a successful bonding. The youngest was said to be working in hotel management in Seattle.

As mentioned earlier, I met one of the sisters. The Anjou Bakery, named for the leading local pear variety, was off U.S. 2/97 on the east edge of Cashmere. On a Sunday morning in October 2004, long after I was no longer working on the Smith story, I was talking to the young woman behind the bakery counter. During our conversation, it dawned on me that the slim, good-looking, very pleasant and obviously intelligent 18-year-old was Bill Smith's youngest daughter, Margaret. I knew who she was, but she didn't know me or that I was acquainted with Bill Smith. My feeling was I had given up the writing project, so why introduce an unpleasant topic.

In a month she was headed for Oregon to study at a culinary institute, and was looking forward to the experience except for one requirement–which was to kill a duck and cook it. I asked if she were a vegetarian. She wasn't.

She added a comment, which baffled me for a second or two. "My dad's a butcher," she said. All I could think of was Bill Smith's harrowing testimony about how he had killed his ex-wife, this girl's mother, with a knife, and his belief that since he had been a meat cutter experienced with a knife, he had spared his victim a lot of pain and allowed her to die quickly and painlessly.

" ... and I knew the knife was quick and fast ... I just wanted it over with, and I wanted it as easy as possible."

For a second or two, I was so confused I wondered if this girl were making a macabre joke about Bill Smith who had, in fact, butchered her mother. Fortunately, I quickly realized she was referring to her adoptive dad, who was a butcher, one who worked behind a supermarket meat counter.

When I thought about this conversation, I sensed the sisters might have a story to tell, but not by me.

Another bit about the girls came earlier during a chat in 2000 at the courthouse with Siri Woods, the chief courts clerk, and one of her assistants. They told me that a year or two before, one of the older sisters, college age by then, had come into the office and asked to read the file on the Smith case, mostly the criminal file. She wanted the information for a college paper.

"She was blonde and smart," the assistant said. "When she came in, she said Bill Smith was her father and he killed her mother."

Siri Woods, who was present, said the young woman reminded her of Bill Smith. "She was focused, single-minded, confident."

The clerk's office was a gold mine of anecdotes and good quotes, some connected to the Smith story and others to the history of recent crime in Chelan County. I spent hours at the microfilm reader wading through the deep file Smith v. Smith, and naturally had many conversations with the helpful women who worked in the office, especially Siri Woods and Joyce Riesen, the assistant clerk and the wife of prosecutor Gary Riesen.

(Bill Smith told me once he liked Joyce Riesen, a woman he considered professional and "a nice person.")

Violent crimes were not unknown in Cashmere and Chelan County, generally involving members of the same family. A husband told his wife that if she got their house in a divorce, he would make sure "it was an Italian-style divorce," meaning one of them would be dead. After a divorce hearing went against him, within 30 minutes he had killed his wife. In another case, a wife threatened divorce. Her husband took out a large insurance policy on her life. He shot her in what at first was thought to be a hunting rifle cleaning accident. The most macabre homicide occurred when a man beheaded his mother with a machete, then sat on the street curb in front of their house and waited for the police.

Siri Woods was not reluctant to talk about the Smith case, including a willingness to discuss the personalities of those involved, including judges. A vigorous professional, Chelan County clerk since 1977, she had been dealing with the Smith case from the divorce and child custody filings to the criminal trial, conviction and sentencing.

The clerks were familiar with Bill Smith because of his frequent visits to their office, often asking for assistance in dealing with civil court procedures and rules, particularly during his long periods of acting as his own attorney. Woods and Joyce Riesen agreed that Smith was smart and courteous, but also arrogant and single-minded. When it came to his crimes, they viewed him as a man "who said he had a job to do, who did the job and did not expect to get away." Occasionally, these descriptions were expressed by the clerks and others, in a form of low-key and almost reluctant respect, not for what he had done, which was cold blooded and criminal, but for his lack of pretense, for lack of a better term.

Siri Woods, in particular, maintained a serious interest in what I was doing, and often came up to me at the microfilm reader wondering what stage I was in and then talking more about her views of Smith. She said, at times, Smith did remind her a bit of a terrorist. She seemed to be impressed intellectually by his ability to follow through on his convictions, a man who did what he said he would do and then took his punishment, a willingness to sacrifice himself for what he considered a better future for his daughters. Her comments were not far from the closing trial arguments of Smith's attorney, Dan Arnold.

Smith's crimes, of course, were greeted with horror by most people, but others inserted a modicum of, not exactly sympathy, but a hint of understanding or compassion. For instance, one woman, the wife of a lawyer, asked me how Smith was doing in prison. I told her he was coping and she seemed genuinely pleased. She went on to say everybody has experienced bad times and emotional strain. "A lot of people don't like lawyers, including me," she added. The woman was less compassionate when I told her Smith expressed no remorse. She didn't like that aspect. Her general attitude was definitely a minority one, but was not all that rare in my conversations with people familiar with the Smith story.

Siri Woods was acquainted with Bob Smith, Bill's brother, who had installed an irrigation system in her yard. Bob was a quiet man, she said, much more so than his brother. His only comment to her after the homicide was, "Bill did what he had to do."

Once, wandering barefoot (because of a foot injury) around her office, Woods stopped to chat and said she was amazed at how "respectful" Smith was during numerous child custody hearings. "He must have been seething under his outward composure," she said.

She also said she thought the Smith dispute "was hopeless from the start," and that both parties were "exceptionally stubborn and beyond reason." Some attorney, she said, should have taken Ann Smith to a backroom and insisted she drop the court fight.

"She was getting married again. She should have backed off and gone on with her life."

This is when she said: "If you are playing Russian roulette, don't pull the trigger."

Woods assumed, eventually, Ann's daughters would have come around to her after they were grown. Bill was a good father by all accounts, she said. He did not abuse the girls and was very committed to them, "maybe too attentive, as in smothering."

She also told me there was no way Smith would allow his ex-wife to be important in the girls' lives. "He loved them completely, at the expense of all else … He was a man who always had to be in control."

Even though she had seen Ann Smith dozens of times in court, Woods had not much memory of her. "She had long hair. She was quiet and thin. I didn't have much of an impression of her. Few memories."

Woods' overall impression after years in courthouse business was that domestic disputes, specifically divorces and child custody fights, "are the most dangerous of all. They are bitter and occasionally you run across people like Bill and Ann who simply will not give up, ever."

She was not surprised at the way the Smith conflict ended. "I could always tell when a man was dangerous. It was a certain sensation when he walked into a courtroom. In Smith's case, it was no surprise that he murdered his ex-wife."

I wondered why Judges Bridges and Small seemed to get the brunt of Smith's criticism, while Judge Cone escaped intense dislike. Cone had called him "evil and manipulative," but Bridges' decisions in the divorce and child custody disputes generally favored Smith. Woods told me she thought Judge Cone was the most "empathetic" of the judges. He could see both sides, she said, so he could get away with calling Smith "evil and manipulative," because he also said Bill was "a good father." Judge Bridges, on the other hand, was blunt and may have told Smith, "Here is the law. This is what you must do."

In addition, there was the matter of Judge Bridges marrying Sue Clem, a woman Smith considered an enemy. In an affidavit, Smith had alleged she and some women friends considered him "a Nazi." Bridges' marriage, for Smith, amounted to conflict of interest.

I interviewed Judge Cone in 2000 after he retired. Judge Small did not respond to interview requests. I also wrote Judge Bridges asking for an interview, but received no response until one day he appeared in the court clerk's office and Joyce Riesen introduced me. Bridges looked like a judge, distinguished and well dressed in casual tweeds. He wore a small earring on his left ear lobe.

"I got your letter. I'll shake hands but I don't want to talk about Bill Smith. Talk to Joyce," he told me with friendly finality and walked away.

Chapter 8
Lawyers and Judges

Lawyers and judges loomed large in Bill Smith's deep antagonism when it came to what he called "the Chelan County cesspool of justice." It was important to include a few of these officers of the court in the story, since they were directly linked with Smith v. Smith and later events. By 2000, years had passed. Memories turned cold, but generally all that was required was a little time and all concerned got up to speed. For instance, Judge Charles W. Cone, retired from the bench, told me when I called, "You have caught me in the springtime of my senility." With some prompting, though, he remembered very well.

Some did not respond or, like Judge John W. Bridges, declined an interview. I particularly wanted to talk to lawyers Chancey Crowell and Steve Richardson, both intensely disliked by Bill Smith and reportedly on his list of lawyers to hunt down with consequences unknown. Unknown because Smith was arrested before he found them. Judge T. W. Small, who had signed the order to send Smith to jail for contempt of court, an order Smith ignored, did not respond to my queries.

Chancey C. Crowell had been one of Ann Smith's several attorneys, but had aroused Smith's anger more fiercely than usual. The men had exchanged personal insults, in court filings and letters. Crowell accused Smith of a "vendetta" and criticized his "sarcasm" and personal attacks. Smith, in turn, in court filings, said Crowell "distorts facts and information" and was frustrated because he had not been able "to stick it to Bill Smith in the divorce proceedings." Smith accused Crowell of "long hostility" to the Smith family "since the Smiths beat him in the early 1970s in a land court battle in Brisky Canyon."

The attorney, Smith said, kept friction "white hot between Ann Smith and William Smith" so he could "milk even greater fees" from the court battles. Crowell accused Smith of "vindictive flaunting" of court orders. Attorney Crowell did not respond to my letters and telephone messages.

One attorney who did respond was Steve Richardson, the court-appointed guardian for the four Smith girls during the court fights. He was a vehement critic of Bill Smith. During their poisonous exchanges, Richardson said Smith possessed "a deep-seated, vengeful hatred toward Ann Smith." Smith said Richardson was "a leech" and was "padding" his legal bill. It was no surprise that Richardson's name, reportedly, also appeared on Bill Smith's hit list. Richardson, the son of George Richardson, retired editor of *The Wenatchee World*, had moved to Salem, Oregon, when I reached him by telephone in November 2000. He was abrupt, unfriendly and skeptical, until I explained what I was doing. He seemed to turn a bit warmer when I said I was an ex-newspaper reporter. Possibly, he figured reporters or ex-reporters routinely brought up unpleasant subjects and nothing personal was involved. He agreed to give me his home address and respond in more detail later if I sent a letter.

I told him I had visited Smith twice at the state penitentiary. Next, as an apparently off-hand remark, which became one of the most memorable of the Smith project, Richardson asked me: "Did he get the jar of Vaseline I sent him? You can tell how I feel about him."

Richardson did not respond to my subsequent letter. I didn't talk to him again.

Two attorneys who did respond were Kyle Flick and Dan Arnold. Flick had been one of Smith's attorneys during the divorce/custody ordeal and was one lawyer who avoided Smith's unrelenting hostility. Dan Arnold, as Smith's public defender in the murder trial, probably was the attorney closest to Smith. Smith's views of Arnold were mixed, but on balance seemed positive.

Flick, who represented Smith from July 1988 until the end of December 1989, told me during a telephone conversation early in 2002 that "Bill

Smith was very caring about his kids. But I knew right away there was bad blood between him and his wife.

"It was a bitter divorce and unusual in that, among cases that go to trial, it is unusual that the mother does not get primary custody. In most cases, the husband does not become the residential placement parent. Bill was very involved with his kids, and the court's psychiatrist agreed. The mother was overwhelmed by the four daughters."

(Flick said the term "residential placement" is used instead of "custody." Custody is "a weighted term that seems to make matters worse during court hearings.")

"I don't remember Ann too well. She had an accent, and seemed like a fairly nice lady. But, it was clear the two of them, Bill and Ann, fueled each other in a bitter dispute."

Flick did not recall any judicial unfairness against his client. He did say cases tend to get "pigeon-holed" by judges and court commissioners and it may appear that not a lot of personal attention is involved. I asked him specifically about Judge Bridges, Smith's priority target in the Chelan County justice system.

"To my mind," Flick said, "Judge Bridges acted courageously in his decision to allow Bill residential placement after the divorce. It was a thoughtful decision. He did not back away."

Judges Bridges, he added, certainly saw "why Bill may not be a fine example of a human being, but in spite of his actions, he was the better parent."

Personally, Flick said, "I saw him as a tenacious person who felt he was the better parent and felt his wife was not capable of being with his kids."

"He was a tenacious man, more so than most, but I never saw a killer or obsessive behavior. Something must have happened to make him delusional. I have wondered what triggered his actions," the attorney said.

Flick said sheriff's deputies told him his name was on Smith's "list," and Flick decided to leave town for a while. "It was quite a time in Cashmere. People were driving around with guns in their cars. It was tumultuous."

In a letter to me from prison, Smith referred to the attorney "as good old Kyle Flick ... he had worked very hard for me." In a later letter, Smith wanted to make sure I had not "lumped good old Kyle Flick in with some of those other sorry buzzards; I would hate to see him painted with the same sleazy brush as those others. Please go back through your notes and you should see that I've always detailed that Kyle Flick then as now had my respect and admiration!"

I reached defense attorney Dan Arnold in September 2011 by e-mail at his law office in Richland. My message to Arnold reviewed Smith's status and included some remarks Smith had made to me about Arnold, including Smith's comment he had liked Arnold and appreciated his efforts, but did not want to be defended. Smith said Arnold was a lawyer, and a court official and therefore "part of the people's problem." He said Arnold tried "to put words in my mouth and get me to say things I didn't want to ... but I kept disappointing Arnold by shaking my head and telling him that I was only doing what I thought any hard-working father would do for his beautiful and precious children."

Smith also said he thought Arnold had taken "a lot of crap, both personal and professional, from Chelan County because he got along with me and kind of stood up for me. I understand Dan has not had an easy time since that time and my heart goes out to him."

In Arnold's e-mail reply, he said the comments I had relayed to him "certainly sound like Bill, although I have no idea what he is talking about my not having an easy time since then."

Arnold is a busy criminal defense lawyer. He has defended several capital murder clients and helped them avoid the death penalty, he said. One case reminded him of Bill because the defendant thought he was doing the right thing to defend his children and, like Bill Smith, did not expect to survive.

"It's true that Bill Smith was not much interested in his defense. As I recall, he reluctantly agreed to let me present an insanity defense."

"Given Bill's opinions about the legal system, it is amazing we got along so well. The day of his sentencing, I spoke to him later and he grinned and said something about the day not starting well, getting sentenced to 125 years, but that it ended up well because that afternoon (at the jail) he had won three straight games of Ping-Pong. That's Bill. His sense of humor was almost always intact."

Arnold concluded his message with a comment that was similar to the direction of his final argument in Smith's trial. "Given what Bill believed, his actions in the murder and assaults are not without their heroic elements. He certainly did not act for personal gain of any kind, except the satisfaction that in his own mind he was doing the best he could for his children."

I was somewhat surprised when retired Judge Charles W. Cone graciously agreed to meet me for an interview. Judge Cone had written intensely critical opinions of Bill Smith, but then decided to let him remain as his children's primary parent. Cone retired from the bench in 1991. I interviewed him in late 2000 at his law office in Wenatchee. At first, he had trouble remembering details of the Smith case, but recovered details rapidly as we talked.

A few months later, I talked to Carol Wardell, the judge in Smith's criminal trial. Wardell, who was appointed to Cone's judgeship vacancy in 1991, left the bench in early 1998 to become legal counsel for the Chelan County Public Utility District. Both Cone and Wardell were helpful and relaxed, a far cry from the often imperious demeanor of judges when wearing judicial robes and sitting on the bench.

Cone's law degree was from the University of Montana. He practiced in Missoula for a while, moved to Wenatchee, where he was the county prosecutor for a few years, then a court commissioner and finally a Superior Court judge in 1978.

Cone was 75 when I met him at his law office in Wenatchee, friendly and willing to talk at length about the Smith case, which had been in his court in 1991, not long before he retired. The proceedings came back to him easily, with a few key reminders. He said Smith v. Smith was a remarkably difficult case, and Bill Smith personally was "at the top of the scale" when it came to difficulty. In his written opinion in the Smith custody dispute, the judge used adjectives such as "mendacious, deceptive, manipulative and unfeeling," to describe Bill Smith, but then said the best interests of the children persuaded him to allow them to continue living with their father.

He told me a judge must weigh all factors. "The children were successful in school, well nourished, well housed. They did not seem to be overly-nervous or downtrodden. They were not shy or withdrawn."

"The test, in a custody case, is which parent would best serve the welfare of the children," he said. "Smith learned that early. The sole problem (for Smith) was Ann. PMS, the abortion, her lack of ability to care for the children. But, he drove her into a mental state where she was almost nonfunctional at times."

"It seems to me, my last impression of her was when she was in court and almost unable to function; she was so beaten down she was almost unable to answer questions, frightened and intimidated right in the courtroom. It could have been the court's presence too. Some people have said I was a little gruff."

Cone remembered that Smith acted as his own attorney much of the time. "I got along pretty well with him, even though he was an ass. I would smile at him, tell him to wait his turn. He would listen to me. He was reasonably respectful. I think he had been in court so many times he had learned what the law was. He more or less knew court procedure." Cone said Smith, because of his military experience, was familiar with chain of command principles.

I asked Cone, in hindsight, what might Ann Smith have done to protect herself in both the custody fight and from Smith himself. Ann, he said, was not capable of acting as her own attorney. As it was, the financial burden on her was crushing. He advocated the creation of civil advocates, which would be similar to public defenders in criminal cases.

"She did the best she could do. We were dealing with a person, Bill Smith, well, I don't think any judge ever got through to him."

Cone speculated that perhaps a psychologist or psychiatrist should try to study Bill Smith while he was in prison. It was Cone's feeling that Smith may have a peculiar form of insanity that has not been named yet. He wondered if Smith were the type of person, who, if he remained in control, functioned well. "But, when the control slips, they do violent acts."

The best interest of his children "really was to have a meaningful relationship with their mother," Cone said, but Smith could never let that happen, since it was necessary for him to be in total control.

The judge asked me if I knew if Smith had ever admitted fault. I couldn't think of examples, except for blaming himself for not preventing Ann Smith's abortion and for not acting sooner to settle matters, meaning to kill his ex-wife.

Asked if there were any solution to implacably bitter cases like Smith v. Smith, Cone said, "The answer is that in a lot of cases there is no solution, no good solution … . If someone has to die to solve it, that means there is no solution to begin with. We could have tried foster care. Neither of the Smiths was really a good parent. There is a kind of a rule that the worst natural parent is better than the best foster parent. I don't think that is true at all. There are some wonderful foster homes. But in this case, Bill would not have let the foster home work either. Maybe Ann wouldn't either. I don't know. She probably would have accepted it with visitation."

I asked him about Siri Woods' notion about not pulling the trigger if playing Russian roulette, stepping aside until the girls were older, letting Bill have them until they were grown.

"Yeah," Cone said, "but you are saying a woman should give up association with her own children. That is hard, not practical. A lot of men would be happy to give up, especially if they didn't have to pay."

Cone mentioned his decision favorable to Bill Smith in the custody fight had meant a sad personal loss for him. Bill Barnett was the father of Rebecca Hovda, friend of Ann Smith and one of Smith's shooting victims. "Bill Barnett was bitter about my decision. He had been a good friend and client."

I asked Cone if he had left town while Smith was on the loose.

"The sheriff's office called me that night and told me Bill Smith was out shooting people and I was on his list. I asked my wife if she was worried. Should we go? She said no and said we should go back to sleep. So we did."

I told him the list so often mentioned was missing. Cone laughed at Smith's speculations the note had been suppressed. "No officer would have any reason to suppress the note, but it surely would be interesting, if true."

(Prosecutor Riesen told me he recalled the list of names was kept out of the trial because it could have been viewed as inflammatory and possibly would have prejudiced the jury. He definitely remembered the list, which probably was found in Smith's pack. It was part of a small notebook with three or four names on it, including, he thought, Judge Bridges and a couple of attorneys.)

At the end of our two-hour conversation, it was clear that Judge Cone had not changed his opinion from 1991 that Smith was the most self-centered and selfish person ever to appear before him in 23 years of hearing domestic conflicts. Cone said to call him any time if I had questions.

Judge Cone died in 2009 at age 84.

I met Carol Wardell in early January 2001 at a coffee shop on Wenatchee Avenue down the street from her office at the Chelan PUD. This public utility district was known at one time "as Kuwait on the Columbia" because it operated three hydroelectric dams on the Columbia River and was coining money by selling power at premium prices during the 2000-2001 electricity shortage crisis in California. At first, when I called her, she was hesitant to talk about Smith's trial. "To tell the truth, it was a long time ago. I have distinct impressions of Bill Smith, but perhaps am short on details." She agreed to meet "for a Pepsi or coffee or lunch," but not at her office. She said her job as the PUD's general counsel was part of her "other life" and she wanted to keep it separate from her days on the bench. Wardell left her Superior Court position in early 1998 after seven years. At the time, she said her decision to quit was motivated by a desire for a new legal challenge.

Beyond the legal challenge, she told me, the PUD position meant "more pay, more time off, less seeing the bad side of people and the bad side of life, every day." In other words, "a better job."

During the coffee shop interview, Ms. Wardell laughed a lot and seemed very good natured. It was immediately clear, though, she had not changed her mind about Bill Smith, a convicted murderer she had called "frightening," as well as "evil and manipulative" before she sentenced him to 125 years in prison. Her hope, she said at his sentencing hearing in 1992, was that he would never be released and would serve his sentence in a maximum security prison.

For his part, Smith showed zero respect for Judge Wardell, going so far as to doubt she was "a real judge" and suggesting in his appeal that she "was closely linked" to lesbian activities, meaning, he said, "sporting organizations." Ms. Wardell had coached girls' soccer and basketball teams. It was not abundantly clear why Smith brought up this subject, except for his allegation the judge wanted to conceal information of this sort from the jury. I showed Wardell the lesbian references in Smith's *pro se* appeal document, which included his speculation that Rebecca Hovda had "recruited" his ex-wife into a "lesbian/homosexual lifestyle."

After reading the relevant parts, Wardell laughed loudly, and said she couldn't remember reading the brief, but did remember the appellant court decision, which affirmed Smith's conviction and sentence.

"Well, I've never seen that before. It's ridiculous."

I wondered why Smith might have brought it up.

"Who knows why he does anything? I never knew why he did anything. Why he made the allegations he did. I think he was trying to smear everybody … No, I never saw that. It's interesting. I'm glad I didn't, to tell you the truth."

Her memories of Smith on trial remained strong, she said. "I remember he was very defiant. Everything he had done was right. He was unapologetic. How awful he thought Ann was. He was protecting his children. He was so sure of himself, that he had done the exact right thing. He had no recognition of the harm done to his children. No recognition of their pain."

Could the courts have done more to protect Ann from a vengeful Bill Smith?

"Quite frankly," she said, "and this is a struggle for every judge, and I had nothing to do with the civil cases, divorce and custody, but part of the struggle for the court is how to protect victims of abuse. You can give them protection orders, but you cannot assign a police officer to protect them every moment of the day."

Basically, people have to protect themselves, somehow. Unless a person makes outright threats, there is little a judge can do, she said.

"Bill Smith was smart. If he had made an outright threat and immediate bodily harm is indicated, there are ways to charge someone with harassment. But, that's a misdemeanor, usually. You can have felony harassment, but then it's up to the prosecution rather than a judge doing it on his or her own because they have seen something in court."

"The trouble is that so much of the time the court is involved at the end, at the time you can't do a lot pro-actively to help a situation. Judges are dealing with the results of years and years."

Wardell didn't see much that Ann Smith could have done to prevent what happened to her. She didn't think a gun in the house would have been effective because "a lot of people have guns and they still get killed."

"And, she wanted to live here so she could be around her children."

I said Ann Smith had told her new husband she feared Bill would kill her if she continued to fight for custody. "Yes, he did kill her and took a lot of pride in it."

Before we parted, I asked if she had had been warned when Smith was at large.

"Actually, the police tried to warn me, but I had my telephone turned off. I didn't know about it until I came to work the next morning. Judge Small was the current judge. I had never been involved, thankfully, in the divorce or custody disputes. I refused to go into hiding."

Chapter 9
Survivors

It took only a few telephone calls to set up interviews with Bill Smith's three shotgun victims. My assumption had been that Rebecca Hovda and Duane and Jane LaVigne would be reticent, perhaps fatigued with the subject of their near-death at the hands of Bill Smith. All were surprisingly willing to tell their terrifying stories one more time. All lived in the same houses in Cashmere where Bill Smith with his shotgun had found them early on the morning of March 6, 1992.

I met Ms. Hovda early in my Smith undertaking, July 2000, before I had moved back to Cashmere. She was helpful, but told me she didn't want to talk too much because she was writing her own book about her experience, which she wanted to write "for the healing effect." She thought writing a book might help her understand better what happened.

Rebecca Hovda was an imposing woman, not at all petite, with long blonde hair and very fit looking. She had a commanding manner, but was congenial and seemingly good-humored. She had a degree in early childhood development and child psychology from Washington State University.

My own knowledge of the case was sketchy then, so our conversation was more about what happened, like a police report, than it was about anything deeper and personal. The details were in her trial testimony. She also talked a little about her close friendship with Ann and her occasional conversations with Bill Smith.

She did say Smith (she usually referred to him as "Bill") was smart and could be charming, but he was arrogant and thought he was smarter than most people–a fairly typical description of Smith by people who knew him but did not much like him. She said the question of how dangerous he might be came up at a Christmas dinner in 1991 with Ann and her husband-to-be Bob Patrick. Hovda's husband, Gary, wondered if Bill were a threat. No one had an answer.

She talked a little about her husband, an interior designer and consultant, who had clients throughout the United States and the world. At the time, his office was in Minneapolis and he spent much of his time there. The Hovda family had lived in Mexico for an extended period before moving to Cashmere. Hovda had grown up in the Wenatchee area; her husband was from Lynden, a small town in northwestern Washington very near the Canadian border.

Her short discussion of Bill Smith ended with her saying he could talk forever about politics and philosophy, to the point of driving a listener half-crazy.

Hovda's house was light brown brick, two stories with high gables, four bedrooms. It was built by a bridge builder in 1928, so was very solid with a lot of poured concrete in the construction. The interior was tasteful, immaculately clean and orderly. There was abstract art on the walls, classical music on a CD, fresh flowers in the living and dining rooms. The furnishings included a piano. The hardwood floors were polished and the windows were leaded glass. There was a light and airy feeling, but not much of a view unless you stepped out the front door and then the Cascades were visible to the west.

There was a side door and that is where Bill Smith crashed through and dashed upstairs with his shotgun.

Almost two years later, I met with her again at her house. By then, I had visited Smith twice at the state penitentiary in Walla Walla, which interested her. I mentioned that I still did not have a strong sense of direction for my Smith efforts and once or twice had tentatively decided to abandon the project, at least for a while. I lacked focus and was not interested in "a true crime" approach because these accounts often read like a trial transcript or a very long police report. But, the prison visits had increased my interest, I told her.

Hovda was not surprised that Smith was, if not exactly happy in prison, at least coping well. She assumed he had retained his anger, had no remorse and was still satisfied with the way things turned out. I told her she was pretty much correct. A friend who had taken a prison tour told her he had seen Smith "strutting" during the tour, which also did not surprise Hovda.

She repeated earlier comments that she found Smith "charismatic and intelligent and well spoken." She added: "controlling and manipulative," a man without close friends, without goals or purpose. He had lived his life through his daughters, she said.

During our two and one-half hour conversation during this second meeting I took very few notes. The interview seemed to flow much better without a notebook or tape recorder. Her comments, though, were easy to remember and write down later.

I told Hovda I had read her trial testimony along with the rest of the trial transcript, but thought a long talk with her in person might provide a fuller understanding. I was right about that. She told me the transcript "was flat and boring, but the trial had a lot of sizzle." Smith was fascinating, she said, and it was clear he wanted his day in court. He definitely got his day in court, but she thought the prosecution allowed him to talk too much about his view that Ann had failed as a parent.

She felt no anger toward Smith, which was amazing, but did feel sorry for him. She will not allow her life to feed on anger, as she assumed his life has. Her perspective was that Smith was "a loser," a man who wasted his talents on antagonisms and anger. She had little to say about any possible reasons Smith had shot her, except that she was a strong supporter and close friend of Ann Smith. She had said the same things during her trial testimony.

During my 2002 visit, two of her daughters were at home, the oldest, 29, and the youngest, 17. The middle daughter was in Mexico. These young women were friendly and intelligent, very pleasant and conversational. Hovda was adamant regarding her rule to keep her daughters out of the interview process. With this strong stand, she was similar to Smith, who insisted his daughters were to be left strictly alone.

I put off until the end of my visit what I thought might be a delicate and possibly interview-ending subject, which was Bill Smith's contention in his *pro se* statement to the appeals court that "my ex-wife had been recruited and drawn into a lesbian/homosexual lifestyle by Mrs. Hovda prior to our divorce in 1988 … ."

I bought it up. The interview did not end. In fact, Hovda laughed and said she did not mind the question. Smith, she said, did not understand friendship since he had no friends. She guessed he would jump to the "lesbian conclusion" because her husband lived elsewhere much of the time. She obviously found Smith's comments ridiculous and another example of his "controlling personality."

"He didn't want Ann to have any friends," she added.

Again, I had found Rebecca Hovda, then 54, to be a likeable, talkative woman, forceful, cultured, perhaps a bit elitist. She had high-class taste in material goods, and in appearance and manner was an upper middle class woman, well educated. To be honest, she was something of an anomaly in Cashmere, which was more down-home than elegant.

She did publish a book about her ordeal, *One Shot, A Thousand Holes,* in late 2002. After some ups and downs with publishers (not unusual), she decided to publish the book herself with help in design and production from a firm in Spokane. When I talked to her, ego and profit motives seemed lacking. Mainly, she had told a writer for *The Wenatchee World,* she wanted to tell her story and give a voice to Ann Smith Patrick.

Eventually, Hovda left Cashmere and established a learning center in Wenatchee for children ages 3 to 6.

After my first interview with Rebecca Hovda, on the same day in July 2000 I visited Duane and Jane LaVigne in their house overlooking Cashmere High School. Their one-story ranch-style home was spacious and comfortable with a panoramic view of the mountains to the west. They had lived in the house forty years.

Duane was a small, wiry man, friendly, outgoing and easy to talk to, characteristics predictable in a man who had sold insurance for many years. He was 72. Jane LaVigne was 71, a slim woman, attractive, somewhat less talkative, perhaps more thoughtful and cerebral than her husband. She was less detailed in her responses to my questions than her retired salesman husband, and definitely was less forgiving of the man who had terrorized them eight years before.

Mrs. LaVigne offered coffee, with flavored cream. I accepted and Duane, an apparent coffee hound, jumped at the chance for a cup.

Duane sold insurance to Bill Smith when Bill was in the Air Force, and he had known the man who almost killed him since he was a boy playing Little League baseball. Duane was perplexed by Bill's murderous behavior. "I figured he might fight somebody, but not that he would maim or kill."

Jane was less tolerant. She said Ann was afraid that Bill someday would kill her. "Ann said so," she said. For Jane, Bill Smith's main feature was "an icy anger," and he had a frightening stare. "Ann told me that while he was in the service his acquaintances called Bill 'the little dictator.' "

On the other hand, she said, "Ann was a gentle person, with an English accent."

Their accounts of the early morning nightmare when Smith burst into their bedroom and shot them, putting both at death's door, were similar to their testimony. Duane heard a door open, a man in a dark raincoat appeared in their bedroom. He opened his raincoat, pulled a shotgun up and fired. "I could feel the heat of the blast," and he remembers the shiny end of the barrel, which Smith had shortened earlier that night. Duane did not recognize Smith.

"I can still see the shiny end of the gun. It was funny looking."

Jane saw Duane shot, the flame from the barrel. "I knew it was Bill. His eyes bulged slightly, and he had a fast and jerky movement. I pulled the covers over my head and said, 'Oh, Bill.' "

Rebecca Hovda told me during one of our conversations that she thought if Duane had been in the bathroom or out of the room for some reason when Bill Smith came with his shotgun, "Bill wouldn't have shot Duane. Bill was after women."

I asked them why they thought Bill had gone after them and Ms. Hovda. "We were the closest to Ann in Bill's mind," Duane said.

"We made it possible for her to exist apart from him," Jane replied. She continued, "He was a frightening man. He was very intelligent, and he thought he could outsmart anybody, including judges and attorneys. I would be terribly frightened if he were ever released."

"Ann was a poor, little thing, always in trouble," Duane said. He also said Bill was "at her all the time," meaning he kept her pregnant.

One aspect of the case that continued to upset Mrs. LaVigne was that newspaper coverage made it look as if she were involved in the abortion that Ann had after she left Bill. "I didn't know about it," Jane said. "Bill called me once after it happened and said something about 'You good Christian women helping her murder a child.' " Jane said she told him, "I had no part in it and I intend to keep helping her."

Duane said he didn't think he and his wife suffered any long-term psychological damage. For a time, he said, he panicked at quick and loud noises and was frightened at night if he thought a door was opening. For a while he had nightmares. One aspect of daily life had changed. They locked their doors.

As I was leaving, Duane told me he wondered how Smith was doing in prison. He seemed genuinely curious.

In 2011, I wrote Duane to see how he was doing. Jane LaVigne had died in 2003 and I wanted to extend belated condolences and to find out if her shotgun injuries had contributed to her death at age 73. I also gave him an update on my tortoise-like progress. Duane telephoned after receiving my letter. He was his usual self, congenial and friendly, and appreciated my letter. Duane had remarried ("to a wonderful woman") and was living in the same house with the mountain view. He said he was 83 and doing fine.

Jane LaVigne had died of colon cancer, so he did not think her gunshot injuries were connected to her illness, although he said the fact she carried dozens of shotgun pellets in her body couldn't have helped her overall health. "I carry 30 pellets myself and set off metal detectors at airports," he said. He carries an X-ray picture to show airport security personnel he is not concealing anything illegal.

Duane was glad to hear I had talked to Bill Smith's dad, Bob, one of Duane's insurance agent competitors years before. "Bob's a good man," Duane said. He was still interested in how Bill was doing in prison after almost 20 years inside.

I could not detect any lingering resentment against Bill Smith. Duane seemed to accept that Bill was not insane, but he had been "insanely intent" at the time of his crimes.

Chapter 10
Letters

Bill Smith has a definite flair for language, specializing in colorful invective, some of it possibly libelous and too risky to repeat here. His letters from prison generally have a friendly tone except when discussing Chelan County, specifically "the cesspool in the courthouse." He often says "the worst day in prison was better than the best day in divorce court." His letters are handwritten, neatly printed and easy to read. He is a careful letter writer, always dating them and numbering the pages. He is polite, often writing "over please" at the end of a page. He has a whimsical aspect, often using smiley faces for emphasis. Sports are a passion, especially professional baseball. He plays a lot of softball and soccer in prison, and is acquainted with a number of Hispanic convicts in the process. His sports participation has been energetic and once he broke an arm in "heavy action at second base." He described helping to take a Native American soccer team to a prison tournament championship.

"We knocked everyone out of the Big Yard and were the bad boy champs of 2000. Yahoo." "Wowser" is another favorite.

Most of his prison associates are older veterans. He seems to have a special positive feeling for Native Americans. He admires Asian women. His obvious dislikes include "rich bitches," and overweight people he calls "fat asses, fat slobs." A ponytail on a man connotes "gay." He dislikes married men who hang around taverns or chase other women. He calls them "cock hounds," and says personally he was never unfaithful to his wife although he had plenty of opportunity. "Butt for rent" women are high on his list of undesirables. The letters contain few obscenities. He isn't religious in a devout way, but does admire what he believes churches can teach children about respect and honesty.

At times he would engage in some homespun philosophy, as when I extended condolences after the unexpected death of his younger brother Troy. Smith wrote he tries "not to brood over the suddenness and shock factor of it all, but through the years I have been forced to experience that fact that life is what it is, we are born to die and during the short time that we are alive, life does go on!"

These were impressions gained from more than two dozen letters since 2000.

My first letter in the summer of 2000 was a standard query telling him who I was–three paragraphs. I said I was an author, which was stretching it a bit. I had written a couple of books, which had not enjoyed commercial success. I was a newspaper reporter who became a part-time freelance writer. Basically, I pitched myself as someone who was interested in his story and thought there was a chance it would make a book. I did not go into detail about my previous time in Cashmere.

Smith replied in less than a month. Right off, he was suspicious about what my "real interest is all about." And, he told me "right up front that my youngest child is still under-age and I certainly owe it to her to do everything I can to leave her high school years as undisturbed and peaceful as possible."

He recommended that I read his comments at the sentencing hearing and in the pre-sentence report. He added possibly libelous details about Chelan County judges and social workers. Smith ended the two-page letter saying he was busy with slow-pitch softball. "My team has been pounding these hippies and wiggers, and I am also pulling together my Mexicali soccer team." The letter ended with a smiley face after his signature.

This letter set the tone. It was frank but friendly and did not deviate from what become a standard bitter criticism of what he viewed as unfair treatment by Chelan County judges, lawyers, social workers and counselors. His letters resembled closely his court filings in the divorce/custody litigation and in his trial testimony and subsequent appeal of his conviction.

In another early letter, replying to my request for a personal interview, he warned me he did not "meet people well and don't much put myself out to impress strangers. You may decide once you get here to make it a quick visit and not come back. I have that effect on people!" Smiley face.

His despair about the abortion of the marriage's fifth child remained emphatic. His description of the abortion: "A mangled lump of flesh to be ripped into pieces, thrown into a bloody bucket and flushed down a drain." After this outburst, he said "one person loved her, her father," and went on to say the best a parent can do is to raise and protect children until schooling is completed and they can "go out and start their own mature lives–that's really all a parent can do and should do."

He praised Bea James, who had become the adopted mother of his four daughters, "surviving daughters," as Smith often put it. "No one better than Bea James."

Smith was "comfortable with the idea I am going to die in prison, that I will never get out. I tell guys that I worked very hard to get where I am today. It is easy for me to do time as I have always been a simple person who is easily able to take care of himself. And, I certainly have come to appreciate a daily nap. There are a lot of worse things in life than to be in prison. I long ago decided that if I was not going to be allowed to be a father to my precious children and protect them, I really did not want to be part of that community (meaning society)."

He is happy to let taxpayers pay his way.

In prison, he avoids "druggies, baby rapers, meth cooks, low lifes in general, big-mouth shit talkers, freaks. Sports is a good way to have fellowship with youngsters. Sports build their self-confidence. Old Bill can teach them." He said younger inmates like him, and ask to sit at his table in the mess hall, get on his teams, live in his cell. His teams were known for success in volleyball, soccer, basketball, softball and pickleball.

He concluded one letter by saying he had to rush to play soccer "against 'Me Amigos,' and some of my crazy white boy youngsters are not ready for team play. Being a cooperative team player usually does not lead some knucklehead to come to prison!"

He gives advice to other inmates about the prison system as well as how to handle going to court, something he knew well. At one point, he was roaming the prison as a fix-it man, with all sorts of power tools, even though he admitted he had no skill at fixing anything. Guards like him, and know he is not an escape threat. "Where would I go? I don't want to upset my girls' lives." Guards know he will finish his jobs and return to his cell for a nap.

He never smoked. Never drank much. So these deprivations in prison do not affect him. He lifts weights and stays in "fairly good shape." Other inmates don't mess with him because they know he is fit and will hit back.

He frequently mentioned his bedrock belief that things were rotten at the Chelan County Courthouse, and that my interest in his case might put me in danger. Once, Smith said he expected to read in the paper about a bad car wreck when "a Mr. Steve Sanger was forced off the road and was in critical condition."

Smith loves Christmas, with warm childhood memories of Christmas with his dad's mother, Grandma Smith, who remains his hero because of what he saw as her strength of character and human qualities. He sent me a Christmas card, non-religious. It is the "warmth and fellowship of Christmas" he enjoys, not the religious part. He described the way he and his "ding-a-ling cellmate" hung stockings in their cell, bought small gifts of chocolates "for the fellas." He even had a good word for the guards, who "are people, not stuffed greedy pricks like judges and lawyers." For New Year's, he and the ding-a-ling had smoked salmon on Ritz crackers, Pepsi, barbeque chips, candy and cookies.

He denied accusations from his mother and ex-wife that he was racist. "I served in the military just as I do in prison with blacks. We bowled together, worked together and drank together." He did indicate he had no close personal friendships with black men although he knew and liked a few blacks in prison, both guards and inmates.

Occasionally, he mentioned people on the outside. Al White, "my best friend," Warren Chastain, "a good old guy," and his defense attorney Dan Arnold. He liked Arnold, but "he was a lawyer and part of the problem." He said Arnold asked him early on why he didn't simply run away from the divorce court troubles. Smith said he tried, once got as far as Bremerton, but decided his daughters needed him.

His favorite book growing up was *Drums Along the Mohawk,* a 1936 novel by Walter D. Edmonds, which became a movie in 1939 starring Henry Fonda and Claudette Colbert. The novel depicted the perilous lives of anti-British farmers along the New York frontier during the American Revolution as they fought the British, Tories and Indians. Pearl Buck was another favorite author in childhood, and Smith credits her discussion of Chinese philosophy with teaching him how to succeed in difficult situations. "There's a Chinese concept of philosophy called He Who Can. In any situation, you can find a way, if you have the will, to get the job done, accepting responsibility, being responsible." No excuses. He said he used this approach while an Air Force sergeant.

He occasionally referred to the Air Force as "the Rare Farce," but obviously was proud of his service record. A "huge disappointment" about being in prison is that he would prefer being in "Iraq and Afghanistan trying to knock sense into those savages. America certainly should force Western values on those barbaric tribes whether they like it or not." He wished he could "have been available to go hunt rag-heads in Afghanistan. Those weirdos need firm handling." His reading has showed, he said, that Alexander the Great had the same problems in that part of the world. If things were different, "I probably would be the oldest American driving a fuel truck cross-country there for the military."

My letters to Smith were not as interesting as his to me. Mostly, they were housekeeping type letters asking questions and arranging prison visits. When he asked why I was interested in his story, I gave him the easy answer, which was an honest answer. I said my working life had consisted of asking questions, finding information and writing the blend of facts and conjecture into a coherent article. In addition, it helped if the story was compelling, as his was, with dramatic and conclusive action. I saw no wavering in his belief he had done the right thing, and no evidence of self-pity or remorse. These combined to create an unusual story.

(Another participant in the Bill Smith story, who asked to remain anonymous, asked me in a more pointed way why I was so interested in Smith's story. Why reopen such "a traumatic experience"? What were my intentions? Psychological? To smear Ann Smith? Raise awareness for a good cause, or simply "to feed the Cashmere crowd's hunger for small town gossip?" I replied the book would not be a psychological study and it would not smear Ann Smith and I had no intention of feeding Cashmere gossip. The only good cause that might result would be, unlikely as that might be, reforms in child custody cases that might reduce bitterness and the resulting inclination to violence. My basic motive was journalistic ... the reporter's instinct to follow an interesting story and write it as true as possible.)

Another reason my letters to Smith tended to lack drama was that I often was at a loss to know how much of my daily life to include. I was writing to a man spending the rest of his life in custody. He would never plan a trip to Sicily, let alone drive across the mountains or down I-5 to California. I could refer to books and comment on them. He was a reader and a huge fan of the prison system's libraries, where convicts had as many privileges as any free citizen, including interlibrary loans. He had worked his way through the *Hornblower* series by C. S. Forester, which he first read in junior high. Two other favorites were *Ivanhoe* and *Beau Geste.* "I always felt like I was the little boy in the suit of armor."

While writing one letter, I was about to tell him about a small domestic crisis. My girlfriend Toby had cut her thumb in a kitchen mishap involving a mandoline, a cut so serious she went to a hospital emergency room. I realized how inappropriate and out of balance it would be to describe a relatively minor thumb slice to a man who had killed a woman with a hunting knife.

In June 2002, I wrote Smith at Walla Walla and told him I was putting his story aside, perhaps indefinitely, which implied forever. I told him I didn't want to work as hard as the story demanded if it were to be told well. My energy was flagging. I had no idea if I could interest a publisher and was not sure I wanted to endure the frustration required to take part in the publishing game again. I wanted to get out and enjoy my advancing years. I lacked the horsepower required to finish the course. What I didn't tell him was that I had a feeling not enough people were talking to me in open and honest ways. It seemed the only person willing to really open up and be responsive was the killer, and how balanced would the work be under those conditions?

Another thing I did not mention was a letter from Al White, Smith's buddy from the post office and the man he said was his best friend. I had written White asking if he would consent to an interview about his recollections of Smith and his daughters. By 2001, White was post master in Stehekin, Washington, a tiny settlement at the north end of Lake Chelan in a national wilderness area. White's response became part of the blend of reasons that prompted me to suspend my Bill Smith project.

White wrote: "Bill Smith and I worked together at the Wenatchee Post Office. Bill and I were also friends. I have tried to distance myself from that friendship. I would not feel comfortable talking about his family. I think you would be opening 'old wounds' and it might be better to just let time heal up what it can and just let it be."

"Just let it be" was a phrase that resonated for me in a true and human way. I wrote him back and said I appreciated his honesty and sympathized with his attitude.

Smith replied fairly quickly to my letter about suspending my pursuit of his story, saying my decision resulted in "a sigh of relief." Lots of people, including people in his family, would be glad I wasn't "poking around" anymore. He thought any publication would complicate his daughters' lives. He said I seemed "a nice enough person" and he had told me things he had not shared with anyone. He did want his girls to know, even if he never saw them again, that he hadn't forgotten them and never would. "My love is as great as it was the day you were born and I held you in the delivery room. My heart and love goes with you always and you girls stay in Old Dad's prayers."

He repeated his regret he had not acted fast enough to save his fifth daughter.

"As for me, all is well here at Wally World (just let the Mariner's keep winning). If you get to visit again, great. If not, then it has been good knowing you. Please take care."

Much of the above was taken from the first batch of letters, from August 2000 until July 2002. I wrote Smith in June 2010 to tell him I had experienced a spurt of energy and the Smith Project was coming back to life. I might have the horsepower to finish the job after all. I was not convinced I could interest a publisher, but would try. Would he be interested in resuming our correspondence and seeing me at the prison? By then, Smith was at Coyote Ridge Corrections Center in Connell, Franklin County, in arid southeastern Washington.

He replied in a few days. "Great to get your letter … your letter is a blast from the past," and noted when he last saw me eight years before I seemed to be "running down and sounding wrung out." True. After an unsurprising tirade about "the slimy power groups of the Wenatchee Valley," he said one of his daughters had visited him. Apparently, the meeting had not gone well. "Hard-headed Bill told her the truth and did not sugar-coat anything, so that's where the situation stands." His father's second wife and Bill's stepmother, Delores, the woman Bill admired and called his mother, had died of leukemia. His dad "was crushed to be left alone."

"As for me, I am back to working in the kitchen doing a piddly job (35 cents an hour), exercising and staying healthy. The Indian kids drafted me to their 'Go Native' softball team, so I stay busy. The new prison library is deluxe here. Great for me!"

If I wanted to visit, fine. "I'd enjoy your smiling face!" He told me who to call and noted the best days to visit.

The letters resumed. Zero regrets. No remorse. No complaints about prison life. He was busy with sports, reading, and pursuing various legal controversies with the system, including what he viewed as serious deficiencies in the prison health system. In an early letter of the second round, Smith answered my question concerning his brother Bob, the man who had written so eloquently in the pre-sentence report.

"Brother Bob is a complex and strange issue," he wrote. Smith said his brother had some success in various colleges, including some law school education, with financial help from the family, and got into the private investigator business in Seattle. After that, Smith said his brother "seemed to go over the deep end." I thought that was an unintentionally ironic comment from a man in prison for the rest of his life for murder and attempted murder.

The upshot was Bill and Bob fell out. Bill blamed this outcome at least partly on a class Bob took, which apparently encouraged students to vent "long-held anger" at family members. "The last I saw of Bob, he visited wearing red-dyed hair (what little he had left) and earrings. I just laughed him off and told him he was a big city boy now … I asked him not to come see me anymore."

Bill Smith also detailed a long and complicated story about Bob's wife, Saudi princes, the FBI, a package carried to London, Scotland Yard. "Very ugly," Bill said.

I tracked Bob down and got two e-mail replies, with a somewhat different story. In his first note, Bob thanked me for updating him on my Bill Smith efforts, and offered to buy a copy if a book ever resulted. But, "things have drastically changed between Bill and me, and I wouldn't feel comfortable now commenting about Bill, or the case." I responded by e-mail, thanking him for his polite reply and saying I was disappointed that he was no longer commenting.

The same day, though, he changed his mind and did comment in a longer e-mail. Speaking of Bill, he wrote, "I still love him very much. He has always been my best friend, as well as little brother, and my heart aches for him and his children. I went to bat for him, and put in a lot of hours of begging and hard work, as well as my and other people's money on the line, all to try to make his legal story told, and correct some blatant legal miscarriages in his case and trial. But, I couldn't get any cooperation from Bill himself, of all people! He just won't understand and/or acknowledge what he did to those poor people, including his own wife and children, was so very wrong, and ill-advised as well."

"I firmly believe that there are some very prevalent overriding mental issues involved with Bill, and what he did, that haven't been addressed by him or the state. His refusal is due to his personality, which is one of intense pride and stubbornness, which, of course, is one, if not the most influential reason that Bill is where he's at, but also the state was adamant in refusal to address the mental illness element, as they were terrified that it would in some way mitigate their already obviously open and shut case.

"Consequently, a very disturbed and angry man sits in prison, and will continue to do so for a long time, because he hasn't been able to see the horror and error of his ways. There are ways for Bill to get out of there sooner, but he refuses to admit he did anything wrong!"

He wound up by reminding me that "Bill is very cunning and manipulative (remember I love him), so confirmation is vital."

It was obvious Bob over the years had not lost his way with words. No mention, though, of red-dyed hair, earrings or his wife and Saudi princes. He asked me to stay in touch. I replied, and asked a few other questions. He didn't respond.

One of Smith's fairly regular visitors was his father, Bob, Jr., who lived about 60 miles from the prison. Many of Bill Smith's papers, legal and otherwise, were in a file cabinet, which was stored in a large trans-oceanic shipping container at his dad's ranch. Smith encouraged me to take a look at the file cabinet contents and also to have a talk with his dad. He warned me his father was not particularly forthcoming and might be too reticent to be much help. In fact, when I finally did visit the ranch in April 2011, his dad was very friendly, talkative and forthcoming. Some of his comments are noted earlier in this account.

The file cabinet, besides piles of legal documents from the divorce, custody fight and the criminal trial, contained personal photos of his girls and their friends, report cards, teachers' reports, soccer team mementos, the girls' art work. Also in it were odds and ends of Bill's Air Force service ... medals, uniform patches, ID tags, foreign money from Britain, the Netherlands, Korea and France. The most poignant were a few unopened letters addressed to their granddaughters from Bob, Jr. and his wife after the girls were adopted by the Mr. and Mrs. James. These were marked "Return to Sender."

I asked Bob, Jr. about his son's crimes, and Bill's steadfast belief he did the right thing.

"Maybe that's the only way he can go on. He has to believe it," his dad said.

The worst aspect for Bob was that his son had shot the LaVignes. "They were good friends, good people. Duane and I were competitors, but we were friends. I saw Duane a year ago and we had a good visit. We never mentioned what had happened."

Another sad aspect was that Bob and his wife never saw the granddaughters again after the trial. "We took the four girls camping near Stevens Pass during the trial, which lasted a week. We had a good time. That was the last time we saw them."

In his letters Smith spent a lot of time and space berating Chelan County justice. It took some persistence to get specific answers from him. For instance, I had asked him several times if "something had snapped" the night he killed Ann and shot Rebecca Hovda and the LaVignes. Finally, in a 14-page letter written in February 2011, he answered in his roundabout style.

He knew he could not trust his ex-wife to do the right thing for their girls, and the abortion "proved to me how little she valued the lives of our children." He would have to be "a shield" between the girls and their mother, and that's why the child psychiatrist in the divorce proceeding recommended he should be the custodial parent, he said.

With the March 6-7-8, 1992, weekend coming up and his jail time for contempt looming, Smith said he was "heartbroken" when his daughters, including the six-year-old in kindergarten, "came to me, one by one, and told me they were not going with (their mother) for the weekend."

"Nothing snapped. Nothing went off. I had known that my smart, wonderful children were being ground down and I was terrified what horrible lessons they were being forced to learn as they were subjected to all those runaway court proceedings. The divorce was over in 1989; my children desperately just wanted to be normal children again and left alone. Their mother's problems were not theirs; the children had a right to a good, wholesome, healthy American childhood and life, and I had to find a way for them to survive their nightmare and salvage their remaining childhood.

"No one liked my method, but it certainly was effective!"

Besides asking questions about his crimes, his motivations and attitudes regarding them, I also was curious about Smith's reaction to prison life, how he had "adjusted," how he was coping, how a basically middle-class man, fairly well educated and with a decent income and with no criminal background, faced what was, essentially, a life sentence. Off and on, he replied.

About living in prison, he said people on the outside had "a misconception."

"They liked to use the term 'adjust' in the same way hippies, queens and women libbers love to use 'evolve.' Prison is always a test of wills. Just as weak-minded and shallow people dread basic training (in the armed services) and drill instructors pride themselves on 'molding' new recruits into good little robots, new guys who know who they are and are self-confident and know their role in life power right on through basic training, eat it up and demand more." Smith said his Air Force basic training taught him very little, although he was not one of "the dud kids" who washed out almost immediately.

These comments were typical of Smith's oblique manner of answering. He did eventually get to the point.

"Now prison, I told people on my way into the system that I was the best one to go off to prison ... I had always felt an outsider in my family. I liked simple things in life like sports, fishing and farming, and hustling for money seemed ugly as I didn't feel like I needed much or wanted to jump through hoops to get it. I was the only one to go into the military. I felt no need for self-serving college. I only went to college after the Air Force to get four years of tax-free money; working and the GI Bill together paid very well. I certainly had no use for drinking much and had never used drugs. I could exist on almost any food and possessions meant very little to me. I could care less about music and I can take or leave TV. Reading is a passion and I am so very easily entertained that I make excellent company for myself."

In a 2012 letter, as the prison years rolled by, his attitude remained the same. "All's well with me, Steve. A guy never thinks when he comes to prison that he would stay so busy! At Brisky Canyon, I use to dream of 25-hour days, now in here I get grumpy if I can't work in an afternoon nap!"

Smith possesses habits and traits that allow him to settle for prison life. Not love it. He may be comfortable in the feeling he gave up his future for the sake of his daughters.

Another positive aspect of prison life was, "Once a guy gets to prison he suddenly has got rights again … suddenly you are a human being," not an "unwilling draftee into that courthouse nightmare … of scumbag lawyers and judges."

In daily prison life, Smith has "no dealings with black guys, zero contact with faggots and queers, hold meth lab cooks to the same level as sex offenders and only slowly make friends through sports, work or such. I may know a prisoner for 10 years before I begin to speak with him." Friends are important. "They have your back, and know they can count on you; they are few and far between."

"The worst fights are over homos, so that leaves me out of that as well. I do have scars from standing up to predators … I demand they keep their hands off youngsters and people around me trying to live the right way." Being good at sports and working out and staying fit also are useful traits. "Low-lifes see you are able, ready and willing to back yourself up."

In one of my letters, I mentioned that my girlfriend grew up on the South Side of Chicago in South Shore, a mostly Jewish neighborhood. Her parents stayed, and became good friends eventually with their new black neighbors. Most of their white neighbors moved as the area became blacker and blacker in the 1960s and later. I used the expression "tidal wave" to describe the transformation from white to black. In a seeming contradiction of his comment that he avoided blacks, Smith said one of his friends in prison is "a light-skinned black guy who was one of the tidal wave into the area (South Side) in the 60s, a great guy who today sure wishes he was back there."

In his 2011 Christmas letter, Smith wrote "Ho, ho, ho, and all the best to you and yours for a Happy Holiday Season." He detailed the college football he had watched and was looking forward to the University of Washington Huskies "taking on Rough & Ready Baylor on the 29th in their Bowl game; could be a long hard day for those Dogs." After this warm up, he responded to a comment I had written about how he had "adjusted to the reality of prison." He implied he did not really know how to answer, except to say, "As I've seen, it is just another step in the process of life."

"I love studying history and from the Greeks, Romans and right through today, multitudes of people have been forced to reluctantly finally stand toe to toe with evil, corrupt kings, emperors, sheriffs, judges and so forth in order to protect and safeguard those they love and hold dear. I am only some little guy who had to face up to what those before me had to endure." After that, he swept into a bitter condemnation, definitely not in the spirit of Christmas, "of nasty, ugly individuals who schemed and plotted to kill my defenseless baby."

Again, he indicated his complete belief in the rightness of the acts which put him in prison. "I do 'Thank God' my surviving lovely daughters have done so wonderfully well in spite of brain-dead judges and destructive government social workers … I came to prison with no real inner anger eating at me as my actions really were very cleansing."

Chapter 11
Visits

Bill Smith was the focus of the story. He was alive and well and willing to meet. Not exactly eager to meet, but agreeable. Prison visiting areas were not unknown to me; neither were convicts and ex-convicts. A younger brother spent four years inside at Utah State Prison and I got to know a couple of his ex-con buddies. I had interviewed prisoners, one of them a freshly-convicted murderer, a 16-year-old black kid in a county jail cell before he began a 20-year sentence at the Ohio State Penitentiary. A happier memory was being served by a Hawaii State Prison trustee what was probably the best cup of black coffee I ever drank. Much earlier, in 1944, I had talked at some length with a German prisoner of war, barbed wire between us, when I was an Iowa farm boy on my way from school.

In one of his early letters, Smith warned me he didn't "meet people well" and I might decide in a hurry to make my visit a quick one and never come back. "I have that effect on people." In fact, when I met him for the first time in September 2001, he was reasonably friendly and forthcoming. Normal, really, except for the cold fury that flared when he talked about what went on at the Chelan County courthouse.

Washington state prison rules in 2001 allowed visitors to take notes, but I had to use a pencil stub and cheap paper towels provided by a guard. No notebooks, pens or recorders. The pencil and towels were available because they were handed out to visitors who wanted to play cards and keep score. Money was allowed, but only enough for vending machines. Pockets must be empty. Visitors were ordered to keep their hands on the table.

My first three visits were to the state penitentiary at Walla Walla, a forbidding old prison, sometimes known, not fondly, as "The Walls." After my Walla Walla interviews, I went to a Starbucks on Main Street, relaxed in an easy chair, and wrote up our conversation from the paper towel notes. These pleasant Starbucks' visits provided a profound contrast to the austere prison visitor area. Starbucks was patronized by students from Whitman College, just down the street, one of America's premier small private schools. These high I.Q. students, drinking coffee in a comfortable Starbucks, were a long way from the convict clientele a mile or so away at the state pen.

The first time I saw Bill Smith, he had been in prison for nine years. He was 47, but looked like a healthy 30-year-old. It was not hard to recognize him. He came in with a brisk pace, a hint of the military in bearing. Erect, tanned, and very fit looking. He was neatly and crisply dressed in jeans, green short-sleeved polo shirt, white socks and polished work shoes. He was balding, light brown hair, sharp-featured, a good looking man, confident in manner. He talked fast and articulately. No sign of humor. He was friendly, and shook hands. His first comment was that he was amazed I was interested in his "lowly self."

Only visitors could use the vending machines. He asked for a 20 oz. Barg's root beer. I had a Sprite, a buck each. Then we got down to it.

He started fast, with what became a familiar tirade, denouncing Chelan County judges, lawyers and social workers. He praised his daughters, without any reservations. At times, he became confidential. "Mr. Sanger, one of my problems all my life was that I never wanted to be anything. I never saw anything I wanted to be. I had no calling." He did not deviate in his views, such as his outrage at the abortion and his regrets he did not act sooner "to protect my girls." He had a moral tone, almost righteous, an occasional obscenity. In no way did he seem needy or show even the slightest hint of self-pity or remorse.

During this first visit, I tried several times to get a definitive answer to my question of what effect he thought his actions had on his daughters. "I have thought a lot about that," was the closest I ever got to an answer. He seemed to find ironic solace in saying he had been told by the courts he could not do anything to change his situation. "They said you can't do anything. But, I was able to do a lot and I did!"

One thing I noticed, something that did not change in his letters or conversation. He did not refer to his dead ex-wife by name, only "she, her, ex-wife, mother of the girls."

Bill Smith was a reporter's dream. Infamous and highly quotable. When I left, his last words were: "I don't care what people think of me. I came from nowhere; I'm going nowhere."

My next two visits to Walla Walla were similar to the first. Smith liked to talk and had no trouble keeping up his end of the conversation. At times, I hesitated to ask certain questions, but Smith never flinched or acted outraged or annoyed. If he didn't want to answer, he simply said so. It was rare, though, that he declined. The most sensitive subject seemed to be his relationship with Erma, the Filipina he said he had married in 1991. He admired and respected her and her family, he said, and did not want to cause trouble by giving details of his connection with them.

Over the years, Walla Walla, located in the far southeast corner of Washington up against the border with Oregon, had become synonymous with the Walla Walla Sweet Onion, renowned the world over. The Walla Walla Valley also was emerging as a fine wine region. North of town was the fertile Palouse, famed for high-quality wheat, green in the spring and golden in the fall, with lovely gently rolling hills. The prison, a looming presence at the north end of town, was a dark contrast. Its address, 1313 North 13th Avenue, was appropriate. Such an address was bad news and worse luck. Compared to Walla Walla sweets and fine wine, the oppressive prison was more in tune with Walla Walla's early history, which included the Indian massacre at nearby Whitman mission. This Christian outpost was called Waiilatpu, *the Place of Rye Grass,* a stop on the Oregon Trail. Cayuse Indians killed 14 whites there in 1847, including missionaries Marcus Whitman and his wife Narcissa.

For my second visit, October 2001, Smith arrived in the visitor area in his customary outfit of jeans, T-shirt, white this time, and running shoes. We had a short chat, Smith doing the talking, about the Yankees defeating the Mariners in the American League playoffs. "The Yankees are stronger and older and more experienced and have endless money," said Smith, who paid attention to professional baseball.

After the baseball chit-chat and the obligatory purchase of the 20 oz. Barg's, I asked him why, after four years in medium security, he had been transferred to more restrictive closed custody. The reason was a fight with a Mexican player on an opposing soccer team. "Not really racial, more like a long-standing grudge." Smith went willingly "into the hole" and then to closed custody, which he said he did not mind. Many of his friends were there.

Smith said his friends in prison were older men, many of them veterans as he was. One of them was Tim Blackwell. In 1995, Blackwell, then 47, murdered three women with a 9mm handgun. The victims were his estranged Filipina wife, who was pregnant by another man, and two of her friends. The women were waiting outside a courtroom in Seattle for a hearing to begin in the Blackwell divorce action. Blackwell was sentenced to life without parole.

Smith said disciplinary action, such as closed custody, can mean a loss of "good time," which is time subtracted from a prison sentence. Smith said he had 110 years remaining, "give or take," of his 125-year sentence under the state's complicated sentencing guideline system. If a more traditional parole system did return, with more opportunities for rewards for good behavior, Smith thought he was the type of prisoner who might benefit if he could stay out of serious trouble. I asked him about his assertions at trial that he was hunting judges and lawyers before he was arrested.

"That wouldn't help my case," he said. He was confident, though, that he knew the prison system thoroughly and would take advantage of any possibility.

(In 2012, I spoke with Ruth Perkins, a public information officer for the Department of Corrections. She said Smith's "earned release date" was 2098, when Smith would be 144 years old.)

His only major tirade during this visit concerned his biological mother, Delores Welch, now deceased, a person, he said, who interfered frequently in his marriage, a woman who was accustomed to things going her way. "She won beauty contests when she was young; she was smart and attractive."

He was still irritated by an affidavit his mother filed during the divorce case accusing him of racism and all-around obnoxiousness. "I'm not politically correct. I watched those old westerns, the ones with John Wayne, and I'm like that. I speak what's on my mind. If you are white, you are not supposed to be proud of who you are. Diversity means everybody can be proud but whites. But, if people are good people, I get along. I have friends in here who are Mexicans, blacks and Asians."

Asian women appealed to him. "I find them beautiful and I like the way they conduct themselves." In the Air Force he wanted to be stationed near San Francisco because of Chinatown. He told his mother he might like a Chinese girlfriend. "That was not at all acceptable."

One subject that did not come up during Smith's earlier notoriety was his participation in county Democratic Party politics. "I was the Democratic precinct person for the Mission Creek precinct. I even tried to understand abortion. I am a strong supporter of labor unions." He said he was a Walter Mondale delegate to the state convention in 1984, the year Mondale ran against President Reagan. For a while, Smith considered getting into politics, the organizational end, running campaigns or being a consultant. He didn't think it would be too hard and he thought he had a knack for it.

(In a later letter, written during the 2012 presidential campaign, Smith seemed to be drifting from his earlier Democratic partisanship. "Been watching plenty of politics on TV and it looks more and more that after trying everything else, this country will end up with a Mormon president. Their religion is difficult to comprehend, but Romney seems to be a smart, clean-cut guy with a really beautiful family.")

As I was leaving after our 90-minute meeting, with the guards yelling at people to get a move on, Smith said he wanted to squeeze in a last comment. I had been asking him about how inmates reacted to terrorism, much in the news then so soon after September 11th. He didn't have much to say about inmates' reaction, but did have a personal view. "So, America has buildings destroyed and people killed. But, then Israel tries to defend itself against terrorists, and the U.S. starts killing women and children in Afghanistan. Israel does the same thing and the U.S. says stop. Here's a guy (meaning himself), the head of a family, his child is killed. When does he get justice?"

This rambling comment was an example of Smith's inclination to narrow world events to his personal situation–a penchant for narrowing the focus. Overall, though, he did not seem unhappy. Prison for him was not a hardship. "I am doing fairly easy time … I am not mad at the world."

My final visit to 1313 North 13th Avenue was on Feb. 27, 2002. This one turned out to include bluntly vivid language from Bill Smith as he described the crimes that sent him to his current bad news address. First, though, he ordered a 20 oz. Barg's. I got an orange drink out of the vending machine. He was wearing jeans and tennis shoes and a spiffy green polo shirt. The conversational beginning was slow until I mentioned living in Cashmere was getting on my nerves, a sure trigger for Smith's standard anti-Cashmere speech. He said the town's "negative spell" even worked its way into his connection with the Evergreen Baptist Church.

"I liked the church and pastor, the Rev. Bob Hamilton, but the people were not very friendly." Smith said he was baptized there, even though God was not part of his life growing up. He got involved in the church because of its youth programs.

In the Air Force, his dog tag said: "No Rel. Pref."

He veered off on a tangent about some vague accusations of sexual abuse, and mentioned complaints of nude photos of Erma in his bedroom, cited by social workers as a bad influence on his girls. The topless photos, he said were calendar art, not of Erma. His daughters had asked him what she looked like and he jokingly pointed to the woman on the calendar.

At this point, Smith got serious and replied to hard questions we had not confronted earlier, specifically the details of his crimes.

"I went to the house and stabbed her to death. As long as she was alive the kids would have to make excuses for her. When she was dead my kids would not have to face certain things." He didn't elaborate. "I made sure she was dead before I left that night."

Why did he use a knife? "I was a NRA member, but I didn't want to kill her with a gun and make it another gun thing," and again he mentioned his butchering background and skill with a knife, all in a matter-of-fact tone.

Next, he spoke of the three persons he had shot with the 20-gauge shotgun.

"I cut the barrel off my shotgun. It was almost a kid's toy. I owned it for 30 years and shot birds with it. I used light birdshot. I never intended to kill the other three. It was a stupid charge to say it was attempted murder. I wanted them to understand. They would look at their wounds and know somebody was mad about their treatment of my kids. I wanted them to know their behavior was bad. I shot beauty queen Hovda in the stomach so she would see that mark and think that guy didn't like how I treated his kids."

He digressed, as happened often in conversations with him, and mentioned the list of other possible victims, the list which never surfaced as evidence. "There were others on a list; I'm not saying who was on the list, but if I saw them I would have wounded them too–marked them to let them know how I felt. I would not have killed them." Subsequently, Smith freely admitted judges and lawyers were on his list.

But, back to the people he did shoot with his old 20-gauge, pointblank.

"I shot all three, so every day they would see that mark I made."

I asked how their behavior could have been so bad, he had to shoot them.

"Jane LaVigne told my kids to call her grandma. She was high and mighty, so important." It was evident from his tone that he was still very angry at Jane LaVigne.

"I knew Duane. He sold insurance and was involved in real estate, a sub-divider. I was always under pressure from LaVigne." Smith seemed to think LaVigne wanted his land in Brisky Canyon for development, something LaVigne has denied. Smith never did say exactly why he shot Duane, except to imply he did not like the way the LaVignes gave Ann Smith money and the fact Ann had rented apartments and houses from them.

Another still simmering subject was Rebecca Hovda. "Hovda was disgusting. Fat. She had a spoiled lifestyle. She was vain. Spoiled her kids. I'll make marks on her body."

Until this brief and ugly conversation, Smith had always acted somewhat detached from his acts. His murderous anger flashed during this visitor room meeting.

I had hesitated to bring it up again, but I asked about his belief that lesbianism was part of his ex-wife's life after their divorce. Smith was calmed down and forthcoming. He said any lesbian angle played no role in his acts and he had no sexual jealousy. "Absolutely none."

"This is sort of blunt, but my wife was not good in bed. She had had plenty of men though. Sex wasn't the reason we got married. I wanted children. That's why I left the Air Force after almost eight years. After we separated, she had steady guys in her life. That didn't bother me." However, he had commented often that he was concerned about the effect the presence of other men had on his children. He had no direct evidence of lesbian behavior.

Another rambling monologue about Ann's alleged faults followed ... bad decisions regarding the girls, harsh discipline, taking money from the girls' college funds, inability to write a check properly, overall irresponsibility. Most of these accusations had appeared in the divorce and custody litigation documents, outraging Ann's friends, who said they were exaggerated or outright wrong.

I left the visitor area thinking Smith seemed ready to talk more frankly and openly, to be more himself. I also had a better idea of why, at trial, his attorney had tried the insanity plea. Smith's attitudes about the non-lethal nature of a 20-gauge shotgun, even if loaded with light birdshot, did seem at least moderately delusional.

It had been eight years between meetings when Smith and I next sat down with our vending machine drinks–Pepsi for him, Pepsi Lite for me. Smith had been inside for almost 20 years. By then, Oct. 25, 2010, I had experienced an injection of inspiration for the Smith story and he was at Coyote Ridge Corrections Center, a fairly new prison in Connell in the wheat country of southeastern Washington, which Smith referred to as "Coyote Ridge Rest Camp." Coyote Ridge was modern and new and may have seemed like a rest camp, but I noticed on my way through a locked gate a pile of leg irons in a corner of the gate control office.

Crisp as usual in white T-shirt and khaki pants, he did not look a day older. Smith seemed happy to see me and shook hands enthusiastically. He even had a small sense of humor, complaining about the governor's budget troubles and the resulting poor quality of prison food. Baloney five times a week, he said. My thought was that considering how fit and healthy Smith looked, baloney must be the new health food.

Vending machine drinks had rocketed in price from $1 to $1.50. Prison visiting rules also had changed. I could take notes on paper towels as I could at Walla Walla, but could not take them with me when I left. "Nothing in, nothing out," the guard said. Consequently, it was fortunate that much of what Smith said was memorable. One drawback was the small town of Connell did not include a Starbucks or apparently anything similar for my contemplative note-taking after the prison visit.

I asked him if the years had caused a change of heart. No, he said, his girls now had a chance for a decent future, and from what he knew they were doing well. I could relay some news of them, which he appreciated. He still seethed about the abortion–"the murder of my fifth child"—and blamed himself for not being able to stop it. During this visit, he admitted the names of judges and lawyers were on his list, but he declined to specify. He said he was edgy and overwrought when he abandoned his pickup that night and left some things behind, including the list, which he assumed the sheriff used to notify those in danger.

A detailed diary or journal of the court cases, along with an explanation of what he planned to do the night of March 5-6 also was left on his dining room table, he said, and Smith still was chagrined that no one has ever acknowledged finding this document.

His feelings toward his ex-wife had not changed in the slightest. She remained for him a woman without a first name. A harsh and inept mother, in his view, uneducated, a school dropout suffering from delusions of grandeur. Again, he told me, he was well rested after two days off before the murder and shootings, and everything he did was "careful and considered."

"Nothing impulsive."

Again, Smith spoke with appreciation of the couple who had adopted his daughters, Mr. and Mrs. James, especially Bea James. "An incredible beauty and a nice woman," he said. "Jerry's a jerk, but he had some good points. Steady job, a home, a steady income."

His logic remained cruelly simple about why he had murdered Ann Smith Patrick. The only way, he said, to insure that Ann was not a problem for his daughters and a roadblock to a decent future was to eliminate her permanently. That was the only way to give his girls a chance.

He talked at about 80 miles an hour, mostly coherent and articulate, and much of it I had heard or read before, with more loud obscenities than usual. Nothing about prison life, except the baloney comment and a few gibes about the "tractor-driving potato farmers" who staffed the prison. When I left, Smith shook hands. He walked over to some other offenders who had said goodbye to visitors. It was clear they were all friends. Smith was relaxed, congenial, at ease.

Chapter 12
Afterword

It was October 2, 2009, years after I had put the Bill Smith story aside. I was watching the 6 o'clock news on PBS and I lingered until the last segment, which featured actress Annette Bening. Jeffrey Brown was interviewing her about Bening's title role in a Los Angeles stage production of Euripedes' *Medea,* the Greek tragedy about the princess who murdered her two young sons to punish their father, her hated husband Jason. He had betrayed her with another woman. I remembered the play from college and decided to watch the interview. The theme of marriage, children, betrayal and murder sounded familiar.

By the time the short interview ended, I realized Bening's comments about the play had hit me hard, so hard I was inspired to revive the Smith story. Bill Smith suddenly made sense, sort of. Not because he was a Cashmere version of Medea. He didn't murder his children. He did seem to have acted out of a sense of betrayal, betrayed not only by Ann and the abortion, but also by much of the society he lived in. Medea's goal was to break Jason's heart, to make him suffer "the deepest wound." She called him "the most contemptible of men." Bill Smith sacrificed his future and Ann's life to offer what he thought was a better future for their daughters.

What Smith had done had profoundly puzzled people, who asked, in anguished grief, "Why did he have to kill Ann and shoot those people? Why?" These questions resembled the traditional chorus in Greek tragedies, women who warned, questioned and lamented.

A few passages in *Medea* were an eerie echo of Bill Smith. Jason, the betrayer, said, "If only children could be got some other way, without the female sex! If women didn't exist, human life would be free of all miseries." Medea replied, "To me, a wicked man who is also eloquent seems like the most guilty of them all. He'll cut your throat as bold as brass, because he knows he can dress up murder in handsome words."

Another macabre echo, when Medea said, "I understand the horror of what I am going to do, but anger, the spring of all life's horrors, masters my resolve."

(These quotations are from *Euripedes. Medea and Other Plays,* translation and commentary by Philip Vellacott, Penguin Books, 1963.)

Over the years, I had been running lukewarm and then cold on Smith. I was skeptical about the chances for publication, which is normal for any writer without clout, meaning a commercially successful track record. More than that, however, I was concerned about how to write anything even close to definitive without including the Smith daughters in the story. This dilemma eventually was resolved. But, probably more than anything, I made excuses about getting old and losing my hunger for print. My efforts to pursue the Smith story languished for seven years, from 2002 until 2009.

During those seven years, I played out living alone in Cashmere and moved back to Bellingham in November 2004, to live with Toby in a one-bedroom apartment with a water view along the eastern shore of Bellingham Bay. We lived in the pleasant Fairhaven district, a part of Bellingham, but separate and distinctly preferable, a livable village. I did intermittent free-lance magazine writing on other things, more cheerful work than writing about anguish and murder in Cashmere. I had put the Bill Smith trial transcripts, interview transcripts, notes, his letters, newspaper clippings and a few photos in a cardboard box on a shelf in a storage closet. For some reason, even though I had not done a thing on the story for ages, I kept the papers. Something had whispered, "Maybe, some day … " Then, along came Annette Bening and the cardboard box came out of storage.

During the interview, Bening seemed almost sympathetic toward Medea, much as Euripedes had seemed to be when he had created his version of the myth some 2,500 years ago. The play itself, which had a few parallels to Smith's story, some speeches and the awful violence, was not my inspiration. Bening's careful remarks were.

I recalled a term from my newspaper days, the "jackpot lead," a catchy term for the first paragraph or two that seem to capture perfectly a story's essence. Some reporters, including me, could not get going on a difficult story until they hit the "jackpot," which meant they had found the key, and the rest of the article flowed quickly. For me, the "jackpot" in this case was not the usual first paragraph or two, but rather a sense of a possible meaning for the Smith story, a cruel one to be sure.

Bening's comments were my jackpot lead.

Toward the end of the interview, Jeffrey Brown said, "If you say 'Medea' to most people, the one-liner would be, 'The crazy woman who kills her kids, right?'"

"Right, yes," Bening said.

"So you have to find a way to make it more than that?" Brown asked.

Bening replied, "My hope, it's that there is a logic. It's *a terrible logic,* but there's a logic.

"And I think that, you know, I mean, those of us who stay within a boundary of what's 'normal' don't really know what's it like for the people who cross over that boundary. But I think Euripedes understood, what I guess I feel, is that there is something that happens in those people that is emotionally true for them."

ACKNOWLEDGMENTS

The author thanks all those interviewed for their cooperation and appreciates the assistance of *The Wenatchee World* publisher Rufus Woods and staffers, with particular thanks to Rick Steigmeyer and Tracy Warner. Coverage by ex-staffer Jeanette Marantos of the trial and related subjects was especially helpful. Thanks also to the *Cashmere Valley Record* and publisher Bill Forhan. Vital help was provided by prosecutor Gary Riesen, county clerk Siri Woods and assistant clerk Joyce Riesen. Thanks to Toby Sonneman for her original suggestion, overall support and editorial and technological skills.

ABOUT THE AUTHOR

S.L. Sanger is an ex-newspaper reporter and occasional magazine writer. Mostly, though, he is retired. Sanger is the author of *Working on the Bomb,* an oral history of the plutonium works at Hanford, Washington, during World War II, and *Cedar County,* a memoir of Iowa. He divides his time between Bellingham, Washington, and Southern California.

Made in the USA
Charleston, SC
07 January 2013